Years of My Life

For: My Mother and Father

Years of My Life

*The future belongs
to those
who have a dream.*

Years of My Life

Years of My Life

Years of My Life
By: *HHien Nguyen*

This book is based on Hien's memories

Years of My Life Copyright © 2023

All rights reserved, including the right of reproduction, in whole or in part in any form.

ISBN 13: 978-1-68223-951-3
ISBN 10: 1-68223-951-9

Distributed by Ingram
Cover Picture by: HHien Nguyen
Cover Design by: Ron Mueller

Years of My Life

Years of My Life

Acknowledgement:

To: Ron for helping the design, lay out and publishing the book.

To all family members' input,

I am so proud and happy seeing the book finally being published after years in the work.

Early Fall, 2024
Indian Hill, Ohio

Years of My Life

Years of My Life

Table of Content

Prologue	1
Chapter 1: The Years Before 1953	7
Chapter 2: 1953 1954 Moving from North to South Vietnam	15
Chapter 3: 1954 Our Lives as Refugees	23
Chapter 4: 1957 Saigon, Living at 128/15 Truong Minh Giang	33
Chapter 5: 1958 My Fourth and Fifth grade at Do Chieu	41
Chapter 6: 1960-61 My Early Years	49
Chapter 7: 1961-1962 Returning to Saigon after Nha Trang	59
Chapter 8: 1964-1966 The High School Years in Saigon	69
Chapter 9: 1966 In the Beginning, A Miracle	77
Chapter 10: 1967-1971 Working for USA	89
Chapter 11: 1971 The College Years	97
Chapter 12: 1975 and the Following Years	107
Chapter 13: 1978 Escaping Vietnam	115
Chapter 14: 1982-1986 Cincinnati – Evandale	123
About Myself	139

Years of My Life

Years of My Life

Years of My Life

Years of My Life

Was written in July 8, 2019
Revised 10/20/2023.

Prologue
10/20/2023

I came to the United States in November 1971. Wow, that means I am here more than 50 years already. More than half a century. I was 23 years old at that time.

I have been living in my current house on Hopewell Road since October 1986. That is 37 years already.

How time flew. More than 50 years living in peace without a war. It only happens here in the USA.

Come with me, let's look back to the history of my family.

Years of My Life

We moved from North Vietnam to South Vietnam in 1954 as refugees. In 1975 Vietnam felt to the Communists. That was only 21 years of an incredible journey for my family. My father was often wished to return to North Vietnam. He would take his family back to his homeland. 21 years. A short time, much happiness and lots of sadness and struggle for our parents. As children, we were innocent, happy and carefree. Oblivious to the struggle our parents faced.

When we moved from North VN to South VN our father tried and tried extremely hard to get us some livable housing. Right after arrival at Saigon as refugees we were living in the old opium warehouse which the French built to process opium for the Vietnamese consumption. The French knew that if they gave the colony people opium, they could continue to be their masters.

The address was 74 C Hai Ba Trung Street, Saigon. After few weeks staying there, my father moved us many times from one location to another. We were still without housing.

Years of My Life

Finally, he learned that in Rach Gia, the VN government would provide housing for its employees. So, he moved us to Rach Gia in the Mekong River Delta of South Vietnam.

There we lived in the warehouse of the VN Custom Bureau. Our living quarter was separated from the rest of the warehouse by a half wall that was made out of coconut leaves. We had no electricity or running water and at nights bats flew over our heads in drove. My parents had to put up cloth covers over our mosquito net to keep their dropping from falling on us while we were sleeping.

We had some oil lamps which gave us some light at night. I did my homework under these lamps.

For water, my parents hired someone to fetch it from the nearby branch of the Mekong river. The Mekong river itself is several thousand miles long and flows through several countries in Asia. My parents then used chemicals to separate out the mud that was in the water.

Years of My Life

Life was very basic, we had very little modern material conveniences. We were happy children since our parents managed to feed and clothes us. We were living there for few months.

Then one day my father, a custom official, caught a boat load of illegal goods. Unfortunately, that boat load belonged to the higher up boss of his boss, who was in fact above the law. To punish my father, the official transferred him to Khanh Binh, a very small village on the border of Vietnam and Cambodia. Khanh Binh is a small geographical area which was under the authority of Chau Doc province. It is deep, deep in the Mekong delta area. On the other side of the river is Cambodia.

We lost our younger sister Nhat in Rach Gia. We didn't know what the cause was. One day, she was sick, and my mother took her to the doctor, and she died in mother's arms at the doctor office.

My brother Tan was with my mother. He came home first on his bike. I remember his face was a pale green when he told me, "Nhat is dead."

Years of My Life

I did not believe him. A few minutes later, my mother walked in without Nhat in her arms, and she was crying. I knew for certain my sister was dead.

Then a few days later, people came to the morgue. They put her in a small coffin, nailed it shut. Then they put the coffin on a small cow drawn wagon and took her to a small area outside the rice field and buried her. Only Anh Tan and I went to the morgue to be with her and watch the people put my sister into the small coffin. I remember, her skin was as white as a sheet. She still had on the clothing my mother had put on her when she had carried her to the doctor a few days earlier. My mother did not dare to see them bury her daughter. She could not bear the pain.

Only the people, whom I did not know, buried her. I don't know who they were but remember that they seemed to be kind.

Brother Tan and I followed the cow draw wagon that took her to the field. They dug her grave, put down the coffin, and the women told me to throw down some dirt so I would remember my sister. I followed her instruction.

Years of My Life

I successfully finished third grade and ranked number two in my entire class in Rach Gia. The school had a ceremony to celebrate the achievement of the children and invited all the parents and dignitaries. No one in my family could come.

My dad had to work in Khanh Binh. My mother had many younger children to care for. So, at nine years of age, I walked up to the podium with my deserving classmates to accept the award all by myself.

After I finished third grade, my parents decided that my father would stay and work in Khanh Binh. My mother would go to Saigon and find housing for us and send us to school there.

I passed the entrance exam to Do Chieu elementary school in Saigon and was admitted to their selective fourth grade.

My mother worked hard in finding us a place to stay. Finally, she found the house at 128/15 Truong Minh Giang Street.

Years of My Life

The year must be 1958, 59. Vietnam felt to the Communists in 1975 so that was our house for 16-17 years. We were considered to be lucky to live in the same place for that length of time.

I went to several junior high schools in Vietnam but did not learn much at the classroom. But I always had the desire for learning and my parents were supportive. They had often said, your learning is an investment in your future. I read a lot of books, novels, essays. Later I learned that the novels I read are world class literature. I read the short versions of these books, but those were immensely captivating. I read Jane Eyer, Wuthering Height, Rebecca, The Time machine and even Hamlet in easy English.

In Vietnamese I read Anh Phai Song, Trong Mai, Hon Buom Mo Tien. The author of these books is Khai Hung.

I admired the characters, loved the novels and no doubt I was influenced by the beautiful and inspiring writing.

I had a lot of dreams, one of those was to go to school in the US or some other country in the West.

Years of My Life

The dream of going to college in the US or in the West seemed like an impossible dream. But to achieve a dream, one must first have to have a dream. I graduated from a college in the US in April 1975.

April 1975 is a historic and disastrous date for South Vietnam. When I was about to graduate from the University of South Florida, Vietnam fell to the Communist. I was devastated. I felt like I lost all my family, lost everything I was working for because I was doing a peace game by going to college in the US while the Communist North was doing the war game.

Fast forward, it is now 2023. With Ron's support, I was able to get all my brothers and sisters to the US where they had a chance to be all they could be.

I feel like I have done my best, have achieved what my parents wanted me to achieve for myself and have helped them to fulfill their wishes.

I have lived in Ohio for more than 40 years and my current home is on Hopewell Road. I lived in peace for more than 50 years in my adopted beloved country.

How blessed I am.

Years of My Life

I will write more about the main events in my life latter in this memoir.

Hien, beautiful fall 2023

Years of My Life

1

The Years Before 1953

May 1, 2015

First, Our Mother.

It has been 40 years since the fall of South Vietnam government. It has been almost 40 years since the day our mother passed away. Yet it seems that only yesterday she was still here with us.

Every time I saw an older woman, or someone talked to me about their older parents, I thought of our parents and often asked the question "How old is your father (or mother)?" Then inevitably the next question "How is he (she) doing?" Usually I, then, tell the person that I am happy to hear that his/her parents are healthy and that having parents around is a blessing.

Years of My Life

Secretly I wish our parents were still alive to witness the success of their life's aspirations. Their children grew up and became good people. They would go on to enjoy the modern conveniences such as a car, a refrigerator, a cupboard filled with food which we now take for granted. I have often imagined the faces of our parents with the new smart phone in their hands and how surprised they would be.

Yes, it has been may years of adulthood, but it only seems like yesterday that I was still a child somewhere either in North or South Vietnam.

No, our mother did not pass away. She is still with us every day and still blesses us with many miracles.

Mother was a simple woman with some formal education, yet she was much wiser than many others who called themselves "educated." She gave birth to and raised all of us. We all grew up and become productive and caring people. She is still around with us, an immortal saint.

The Years Before 1953

During the war, our parents were refugees, they had to run, physically; yes, on foot from one village to the next. One night, they arrived at Dao Pho, Huyen Ninh Giang district, Tinh Hai Duong province. That is where mother gave birth to me in a Midwife's house. Mother said that it was just right at the time when the midwife wanted to eat her dinner.

My earliest memories of our mother were the time Khanh, and I went to church with her in the Village of Xam Dong outside of Hai Phong in North Vietnam. I must have been four years old at that time. The Catholic Church and Christianity was brought to Vietnam by the French missionaries. The French then used that as a mean to invade and took over Vietnam. They enslaved us for almost a century. We were their slaves in our very own country.

Only a 'privileged 'few were trained and 'educated' to become the ruling class of the not so 'lucky' Vietnamese. The French were using these Vietnamese to rule the other Vietnamese. In reality the ruling class were not really Vietnamese even though they looked Vietnamese.

The French educated them to embrace the French culture and customs. They were the French in disguise.

At that time, being a Catholic in Xam Dong village was the only way to stay there. If you were not a Catholic, you do not belong there. The Catholic Priest is the son of Heaven. His words are the words of the Lord.

I remember there was no bench at the church we went to, we all sitting on the straw mats for the ceremony. Father did not come with us to church. Remember I wrote earlier that he accepted the conversion to the Catholic faith so that he could safely move his family to Xam Dong and settle down after many years of wondering as refugees running from village to village to escape the war.

One day, on the way home from Church, a Vietnamese guard stopped, Mother, Khanh, and I. I vaguely remember he questioned her about something not wanting to answer him. Mother apologized for not paying attention.

The Years Before 1953

I remember Mother is the one who nursed the huge cut in my foot, a cut made by a piece of broken glass. I was playing with Anh Tan and sister Khanh in the rainstorm swollen mud waters of a rice paddy when I got this cut. This deep, to the bone, cut ran the entire length of my foot.

I remember seeing Mother chew the aspirin pills, fill the wound up and wrap it in cloth. It was probably from a torn shirt. Yes, I recovered and was stronger than ever. There were no antibiotics, no doctor, no emergency room. Mother had the ability to create miracles even years and years ago. The scar from that cut is still on my foot.

Father had a plan to stay in Xam Dong Village. He planted papaya plants and squash, mong toi etc. I remember there was one harvest of papayas, people came and gathered the fruits. Then right after that we had to move again to Nha Be Lai Vien near Hai Phong city. Father was not much of a city person, and he always wanted to settle down and grow a garden.

Years of My Life

I am not sure why we moved at that time. I believe the move was due to social, economic and the changing of the political situation in Vietnam. Staying in one place was a luxury our parents did not have.

Another factor could have been because he was ashamed of his younger sister, Co Them, who ran away with Câu Lê because they were in love with each other and Cau Le was not considered worthy of her in the eyes of the society of the time.

We moved to a few more places in Hai Phong. It must have been Lac Vien village around 1954 because I remember this is the time Mother was pregnant with Thuy. Father built a thatch roof mud house in the middle of the field since he did not want "to argue with the neighbor due to children" issues.

At Lac Vien we had two ponds created due to the building of the mud house, we needed the mud. One pond was used for the water for cooking and drinking. The other pond was for bathing and washing.

The Years Before 1953

I remember across the street from our house is a French military compound. Soldiers came in and out of that compound with their big tanks and military vehicles. Once in a while, they came over to our house and asked for water. We did not have any problem with them. Once, there were many, maybe one hundred of the minority military members and their families. Maybe they were the Hmong and joined the French supported military. They came to our house, occupied the outside of our house, and used our ponds for days or weeks. I do not know why and only remember we put up with them the whole time they were there. Then one day they left with the French military.

Anh Tan, sister Khanh and I attended the Back Dang School in Hai Phong during this time. I remember Father rode a bike and took Khanh and me to school on it. To protect us from the sun we were ordered to wear the 'Non Coi' a Ho Chi Minh type of hat which usually was worn by men. I hated wearing that hat. Other kids teased us for not 'being fashionable.

Father always valued education. Even sister Khanh and I enjoyed the privilege of going to school. Our family was different from other families. At that time, in general, only boys got to go to school. Girls had to stay home to take care of the housework or help the family to earn a living. Boys are expected to carry on and build the family legacy. Since then, I have found this is also somewhat true in Western cultures.

We stayed there for a while. We did have some conflict with the neighboring kids and sister Khanh was always the fighter and protector. I could only follow her.

During this time, I noticed there was a man who probably worked with Father. This man came to our house and talked to Father many times. Later, I learned from Mother that the man came to persuade Father to stay in North Vietnam and not to move to the South. Mother mentioned that this man told Father that he should not uproot his family and move South since the Communist would be there in few years." But Father had a taste of the Communists and decided that he would take his family to the South.

The Years Before 1953

1954 with the defeat of the French in Dien Bien Phu and the Geneva Treaty, Vietnam was divided into two.

One million people from the North moved to the South.

Before we moved to the South, we moved down to Hai Phong to be ready. I remember we live in a government sponsored housing area. It was here that Uncle Hien, our mother's younger brother, came to visit us and stayed with us.

Mother told us that Uncle Hien, at the age 17, joined the Viet Minh in their fight again the French Colonial power and achieved the rank of Captain.

We did not stay very long in this government housing. Soon after that our family were refugees once again, all board the American LSD, and they moved us to South Vietnam.

Years later in 2015, I am sitting in my comfortable house at Hopewell Road and looking back at some of the events that happened to our family.

Years of My Life

Our father was a smart and determined person. He knew that we could not live with the Communist and courageously determined to take his family to the South. He was smart to maneuver that move safely for himself and all of us because the Communists were cruel to people who disagreed with them.

Mother was always a supportive wife and mother. Whatever the reasons, her family was always first and was always right.

Thank you, Mom, and Dad. We will always love you and you are always with us.

Happy Mother's Day, Father's Day and in 2023 Thanksgiving Day.

    Hien May 10, 2015
Note: I finished editing this chapter in November 2023.

The Years Before 1953

Years of My Life

2

1953 1954 Moving from North to South Vietnam

In 1954 with the Geneva treaty, the fighting between the North Vietnam and the French was ended with the defeat of the French at Dien Bien Phu. Vietnam was divided into two countries. Starting from the 17th parallel to the north geographically is the Ben Hai River in central VN, connecting to the South is the Hien Luong Bridge was the domain of the North Vietnamese communist. From then on, they were called North Vietnam. The Russian and communist China supported them.

From 17th parallel to the South was the domain of the regime that was supported by the French and then the Americans.

Years of My Life

Our family history is intertwined with that world history. To understand more, you may want to watch the documentary series; "*The War in Vietnam*," by Ken Burn.

Because our father worked for the French and had experience with the communists, he decided to take his family and move to South Vietnam.

At that time, father was forty-one or forty-two years old. My mother was in her early thirties. They had seven children. The oldest, our sister Tuống died in early childhood. Tan, Khanh, Hien, Hiep, Nhat, and Thuy were the six moving south with them.

Mother's younger brother Cau Hien also came with us. He was a fighter for the North who bravely fought against the French and somehow was convinced to move South with us. More about him latter.

In 1954 we stayed in a temporary quarter in Hai Phong and waited for the day we could board a ship to South Vietnam.

There were two modes of transportation for the refugees to move south: by air or by sea.

1953 1954 Moving from North to South Vietnam

Our father opted for the sea because he said it was riskier to travel by air.

The US provided a Landing Ship Tank (LST) to move the refugees from Hai Phong harbor to the main ship which was docked out at sea. When we arrived at the dock there was a big line of people waiting to board the ship. Father saw the empty opening and directed us to board the ship by that way.

Later on, we learned that if we were stayed in the heavy line with many people, we would have received a voucher of approximately a three-hundred-dollar allowance for each person and we did not receive any of that.

We all felt bad at the time but years later I learned of the tradeoff. People in the crowded line were sprayed with DDT to prevent disease they brought with them. Ah, DDT was an acceptable bug killer at that time.

We finally arrived at the big ship and ready for our three-day journey to the South. We did not know what was to be ahead of us. It was whatever destiny might bring.

Years of My Life

Father did not want us to stay in the hull of the ship with other refugees, he founded a narrow passageway and kept us there. Thankfully, there we could see the sun, the ocean view. It reduced our seasickness.

The Americans gave us hotdogs for food. This disgusted our father with the look and the taste.

After 3 days journey, we finally arrived at Saigon harbor. We were trucked to 74C Hai Ba Trung street. This was the old opium warehouse of the French. It was called Nha Nau Thuoc Phien, "a place to produce Opium." You see, the French did not want us to fight them, so they freely gave the Vietnamese opium. They perpetrated a drug war on the Vietnamese.

Our family occupied a space in the building that was about a twelve-by-twelve feet.

All cooking was done by charcoal in the middle of the building that filled with carbon monoxide.

Filthy common toilets were at the end of the building.

To fit all of us in that tinny space, the authorities provided beds with several levels and DDT was spread everywhere.

1953 1954 Moving from North to South Vietnam

To this day, I still vividly remember the color white of that poisoned powder. It was laden in all the creases and corners of our beds.

My father, who always love education and wanted the best for us, sent sister Khanh and me to Da Kao elementary school. I remember we were in first or second grade. The walk to school was far for our little feet. Sometimes we were given taxi allowances.

At Da Kao elementary school. I was always an awkward girl because of my height. I was taller than most girls and boys.

I had a happy childhood, even at the refugee camp.

Here, I had some friends, but my best friend was always my sister Khanh.

Thuy was a beautiful baby boy and was adored by many of the neighbors. Mrs. Tieu, who lived in the same compound, often carried him for a walk in the evening to Nguyen Hue flower market. We, of course, followed her.

Hiep had a problem with one of his eyes, the lash of the troubled eye grew inwardly and irritated the eye. To protect itself, the eye grew a membrane. I was told the membrane would become thicker and thicker if the eye was not treated. He would lose the sight of that eye. Mother often had to take him to the doctor to clean that membrane. Hiep usually came back with a bloody eye and had the bandage to cover it for few days.

In front of our refugee compound at evening comes, there were vendors in three wheeled carts that came around, selling popsicles or fruits. Nice treat if we had money.

Nearby was a theater. If we had money, on the weekend, we would go and buy the children's standing only tickets. I remember we always loved all the shows.

Across the street from our refugee compound was a row of upscale town houses. There were some French children who lived there. Sometimes we played hide and seek with them. Their nanny did not seem so pleased that they played with the ragged refugee children. But we did not care.

1953 1954 Moving from North to South Vietnam

Further up in the street, in the corner of Hai Ba Trung street and perhaps Gia Long street, was the American library. I loved to go to the library and read one magazine, one and only one, in Vietnamese. I love the rows and rows of books and books.

Somehow the love of books and library was in me. Later on, wherever I happened to be I liked to find a library. I would go there at least for a visit.

In 1956 Mother gave birth to Nga at the birth house named Dr. Ky Quan Than.

In 1958, mother gave birth to Hang at the same place and the same doctor cared for them both.

There were now eight children in our family.

I had to count the number of children again. Kids plus parents made the family ten people. We were all living in the approximately a twelve foot by twelve-foot space.

Magically, I did not feel crowded or uncomfortable. I was just a happy child.

Can you imagine? We lived at 74C Hai Ba Trung for around 2 years.

Uncle Hien, our mother's younger brother, came with us to the South. Remember I wrote that he bravely fought for the Viet Minh and had won many battles against the French. Somehow, he surrendered to the French regime in Hai Phong and went south with us. I understood he had left his wife and children behind back in North Vietnam. I did not like him because once, I accidentally knocked over something he was working on, and he slapped me for that. Ah, the way to correct children is to physically beat them.

Years later, I heard from Uncle Kinh, our mother younger brother, that Uncle Hien went to Quy Nhon to visit with his older brother, Uncle Kinh. He borrowed uncle Kinh's bike and rode that bike to the Ben Hai river or the 17th Parallel, left the bike there, swam across the river and went back up North.

I think Uncle Be, my father's younger brother, was working in Loc Ninh during this time.

1953 1954 Moving from North to South Vietnam

Also, while we were living in 74C, Hai Ba Trung, Co Them, and her now husband, Uncle Le came to visit us. They also had their baby Cap with them. They brought my parent a huge pineapple as a present. Cau Le told our parents that he had a job at the Saigon Zoo.

Our parents were happy for them. Father accepted the fact that his sister was now married to a man he had once disapproved of.

Father was not happy with our living condition. He moved us around to a few places. We shared housing with another family. Then he moved us to Khanh Hoi. The house was sitting on still underwater, that perhaps was an open sewer. It did not work out. He had to return to the refugee compound.

Finally, he heard that the government was offering housing to its employees in the town of Rach Gia in the Mekong River Delta. He applied and was accepted a transfer to Rach Gia.

I finished my second grade at Da Kao school and was ready for my third grade in Rach Gia. The year, then, must have been late 1958 or early 1959.

Years of My Life

1953 1954 Moving from North to South Vietnam

Years of My Life

3

1954 Our Lives as Refugees

Rach Gia South VN 1954

As I mentioned earlier, in a quest to find housing for his family, our father asked for and received permission from his work to be transferred to Rach Gia, a city in the Mekong River Delta. Here, I understand, the government allowed housing and food prices were reasonable. One of these days, I may have a chance to go back to visit this city where I spent almost a year of my childhood.

At Rach Gia, I was in third grade of a local elementary school.

Our father tutored Hiep at home. Every morning, before going to work, father would sit in one end of a small table drinking his coffee, and on the other end was Hiep's sitting place to learn his primary lessons. Our father was teaching Hiep how to read, to spell, and do some arithmetic.

Every morning, very early at dawn, I had the task of riding my little bike to the Rach Gia market area to the bread shop name Quach Xoai to buy a loaf of French bread. The bread store was about a few miles from the house and across the river.

To get there, I had to bike across an ancient temple with a big banyan tree in front of it. This was a giant tree with roots hanging from its higher limps. I had seen many local rituals displayed in front of this temple with people dressed up in some ceremonial form to offer their respect to the long-gone spirits. I was told there are ghosts living on that tree.

Two things I was afraid of the most every morning when I had to bike across the river to buy bread: the ghosts in that banyan tree and my classmates.

1954 Our Lives as Refugees

I was very worried because they would see me riding a little bike. They would laugh and make fun of me since the bike was smaller than I was. But that's was all my parents could afford. One person working and 10 mouths to feed.

Anh Tan stayed in Saigon at Mr. & Mrs. Phu's so he could attend school since school in Rach Gia may not provide 'good education.'

Sister Khanh and I divided our time so one of us could help our mother with childcare and housework while the other attended school.

We did not live in the same housing quarter where other employees lived, instead, our father chose to move us to live in a section of the warehouse, which I believe because it has more space. This warehouse was divided into three sections. We lived in one end section. Another family lived at the other end. The middle section was used to store captured smuggled goods.

Years of My Life

Our father worked for the South Vietnam Custom agency. The job of the agency was to make sure all goods were being taxed. Traders often tried to skip tax payment, so their goods were considered smuggled goods and when captured, the goods were held in the warehouse.

We had no electricity and no running water. For the water, we hired someone to fetch water from the Rach Gia River.

We used an oil lamp for light. We did our homework under the dim light of the oil lamp.

Bats flew over our head in droves at night. Our parents had to use a layer of cloth to cover the bed and hang mosquito netting to catch the bat droppings.

Our father's place of work was in a compound surrounded by a cement fence. Inside, there were many banana plants and guava trees. At the corner of the compound near the path to our humble quarter was a pond where they raised fish. I think the fish were tilapia.

1954 Our Lives as Refugees

The compound also housed the Chief Officer of the Custom Group. This chief really had a lifestyle above all of the employees reporting to him. He and his family collected all the banana and guava fruits, plus harvested all the fish.

The compound also had a giant tank to collect a precious commodity, rainwater. Which the Chief and his family had the exclusive right to use. He and his family also have the exclusive right to the only automobile, a chauffeur, maid, and a gardener. All of those were at the expense of taxpayers.

I remember his gardener, Ong Nam. Our parents hired Ba Nam as a helper to help with domestic activities. Every day Ba Nam carried water from the river and poured it into two four hundred gallon tanks for us to use. She also helped with washing our clothes on the Rach Gia River.

Our lives were very basic and simple. No electricity, no running water, no bathroom. No TV or radio. None of the modern-day appliances. Just like the primitive lives you see in the Our Planet series.

Nga was the smallest child. Poor Nga, she had whooping cough and would often wake up and cough and cough at night. I had often wondered how long that small body can endure those scary episodes. Of course, that worried our parents also. Our parents were only in their mid-to-late thirties without any relatives nearby, yet they had seven kids to care for, to feed, and clothe.

The Rach Gia River is major live blood for the population. Mother went to the market every day to buy food for us. She often came home with a basket full of local produce and fish just caught in the river the night before. Beautiful fat fish from the local river.

For a while, our lives were pretty smooth.

In the evening, I followed the fishermen along the riverbank and watched them throw the net and catch some small fishes. It was the fisherman's way of making a living.

Anh Tan came to Rach Gia to live with us. He must have been 13 or 14 years old. I heard that at Ong Phu's house, he climbed trees and tried to catch birds but fell down and injured himself.

1954 Our Lives as Refugees

In Rach Gia, he show cased his talent in catching sparrows by popping two bricks together with few sticks then he lured the birds in with few wheat grains and when the poor birds tried to eat the grain, the brick would fall on it and voila, the bird was caught. He caught many sparrows this way and often cleaned and then cooked the birds over a small fire.

Fate would have it in its own way. Our family was not left alone to work and to live our lives together. One day, being a dedicated Customs Officer, our father and maybe some other officers caught a big load of smuggled goods. Later on, he found out that the smuggled goods belonged to some higher-up official.

So, he was not allowed to stay in Rach Gia and was transferred to the Vietnamese, Cambodia border to a little town name Khanh Binh. A small village just outside Chau Doc.*

The Rach Gia custom Officer chief allowed our mother and the rest of us to stay in the warehouse while our father worked in Khanh Binh because it is a very primitive town and did not have any type of housing for employees and their families.

Our father continued to work in Khanh Binh and came back to Rach Gia to be with us a few days each month. Mother was alone with us, raising the seven kids; Tan, Khanh, Hien, Hiep, Thuy, Nhat, Nga and she handled all the family affairs.

Our helper, Ba Nam, usually stood on our side of the warehouse compound and yelled at her husband who worked for the chief. This irritated the chief, and he sent our parents a note ordering them not to hire this woman or he would evict us.

I finished my third grade at the local public school and was recognized with an academic excellence award. I was happy to receive it. It was an easy academic year even though the teachers' Southern accents were hard to understand.

The school honoring the best student's ceremony was held at a local theater. I remember the place was full of dignitaries and proud parents. I was the only child that showed up to receive the award without parents or any adult because our father was working at Khanh Binh, and our mother was very busy with several smaller brothers and sisters.

1954 Our Lives as Refugees

*In 2023 you can see many videos on YouTube about this area

As for me, I was not sad and just happy that the school year was over. I had a good year, made some friends and from time to time was teased because I had a Northern accent, and we were in the deep South of Vietnam. They had different Southern accents. This is where and when I learned to speak with the Southern accent.

One very, very, sad, and gloomy day, yes, it was truly a gloomy day. Our mother took our sister Nhat to the doctor because she was ill. A few hours later, I remember Anh Tan returned first, his face was pale green, he was sad, and he was exhausted. He carried his bike into the house and quietly told me that Nhat was dead. I did not really understand the true meaning of what he said nor believe in it at the moment. Was he joking? I wondered. A little while later, our mother came into the house all by herself, she cried and cried 'oh my baby, my baby…'

At that moment, I realized that Anh Tan was not kidding and that now we lost a beloved sister in Rach Gia. I remember many nights; our mother would wake up at the middle of the night for many nights and start crying.

So did the rest of us.

I remember a day, or two later Anh Tan and I went to the morgue. It was a small, simple building at the far end corner of the hospital, to see our sister Nhat.

She was the first dead person that I saw. She was wearing the same clothing that she had on when our mother took her to the doctor earlier. Her face and hands and feet were as white as a sheet of paper. She looked peaceful. Some adults showed up with a small coffin. They put her into that small coffin and nailed it shut. My heart felt heavy, and I wanted to tell them no please don't do that, you'll hurt my sister, but I dared not. The adults then put the coffin on a cart pulled by a cow. Our mother did not come. She said she could not bear the pain of losing a child.

A few grown-ups, Anh Tan and I followed the cart to the field far away. At the corner of that field, they stopped and dug her grave. They told Anh Tan and I to gather some dirt and throw that into the grave, that way, we would not miss her as much.

Our father came home from Khanh Binh after he received two telegrams from Anh Tan, the first one said, 'Nhat is sick; please come home,' the second one said 'Nhat is seriously ill, please come home right away.'

He said his incompetent boss did not let him go home at the first telegram but did let him go home on the second one. By then it was then too. He was very sad and bewildered.

Our parents decided that Rach Gia was not a place to raise the family, so they decided to move all of us back to Saigon.

Years of My Life

1954 Our Lives as Refugees

Years of My Life

4

1957 Saigon, Living at 128/15 Truong Minh Giang
<u>Our Lives after Rach Gia 1957</u>

Our parents moved us back to Saigon, but before they could find housing, we temporarily lived at Ba An's house in Go Vap located outside Saigon. It was a muddy area in those days. Ba An is our mother's aunt. She was a widow living with one daughter, the daughter's name is Loan. We called her Di Loan. She is the same age as sister Khanh but ranked 'Di' because it is the family relationship ranking. The modestly constructed house was built by bamboo and mud with a roof covered by coconut leaves. It was similar to any house in the country at that time.

Years of My Life

It was summertime so we did not go to school, instead, many days, Di Loan, sister Khanh and I went to the Go Vap country market. Here mud usually covered up to our ankles. We bought some baby ducks and tried to raise them.

Living conditions were very primitive but we did have a roof over our head for a few months. In the meantime, our mother did the house hunting. She tried to find a place for us to live and to go to school.

Our Mother also has another aunt, Ba Ly, she lived near the church Dong Chua Cuu. The church is still there in 2023. Perhaps she helped our mother to go to look for a house, which is why we ended up at 128/15 Truong Minh Giang.

Our 128/15 house was a small one. It is four meters wide and ten meters long. If you counted the veranda, it would be fourteen meters. But during the time we lived there, we lost the veranda because it was used as a walkway for the neighbors.

1957 Saigon Living at 128/15 Truong Minh Giang

There were twelve to fourteen of us living in this house. One nasty bathroom was located right inside the kitchen. We also had to have a big open cistern to store water for the day.

Mother ordered and paid for a supply of water which was carried in by buckets from the nearby outside public faucets to our home.

Each of us was given a small towel, the size of a dish towel to use for washing our face and drying ourselves after bathing. One towel and one only. Not one for each day or month, just one towel.

I think that must have been 1958 and that was the year Hang was born. Mother gave birth to her at the same maternity house of Dr. Ky Quan Than on Phan Thanh Giang street.

I passed the entrance exam for the elementary school at Truong Do Chieu near Tan Dinh market and was admitted to fourth grade. I attended this school in both fourth and fifth grade. After that I graduated from grade school.

Sister Khanh refused to take the entrance exam, so Di Loan took it for her. Being in a grade higher than Khanh's, we were sure that she would pass the exam. She did not.

Do Chieu was a selective elementary public school. Students were required to wear a uniform that consisted of a white blouse and white slacks.

Once in a while we received some writing tablets and pencils as a gift of the CARE organization. CARE also donated 'powdered milk.' The students also had to line up for a glass of this awful drink every so often.

In the late 1950's and then 1960's, public schools were ranked much higher than the private (for profit schools)

Every morning before class began, we had to stand and salute to the flag, sing the National Anthem and the Appreciation of Ngo Tong Thong song (Ngo Dinh Diem president). We sang it so often that I still remember the lyrics to this day. The politicians tried to instill that terrible propaganda into our young and innocent minds.

1957 Saigon Living at 128/15 Truong Minh Giang

Our fourth-grade teacher was a middle-aged person. I think they called her Co Muoi. At that time, capital punishment was an acceptable form at school. Whew, I still don't know how the teacher would feel when beating up a student for a mistake they made.

Our teacher, co Muoi, did not hit us but if we made a mistake, we would have to write the correction a hundred times and sometimes we had to pay with money.

The money was then used to buy cloth. Later, the cloth was distributed back evenly to the students.

I witnessed something this teacher did and still remember that to this day. It influenced me on my handling of my kids' their teachers.

There was a girl in class name Nu, she was a quiet girl but not very smart. She always sat at the table at the back of the class. She could not or did not do the homework. So, Co Muoi ordered her to write the lessons many times, probably in the hundreds.

One day, her father, a laborer, who was upset and came to the class and in front of all the students, he confronted Co Muoi. They exchanged loud words.

Finally, the father walked away in angry.

Co Muoi, too, was angry.

From that day on, Co Muoi completely ignored Nu.

At practice math time, the class was required to go up to the board to do our math problems. Co Muoi would tell Nu to "please stay where you are, sweetheart." Co Muoi used her extreme weapon, ignoring a student.

That went on for the entire school year. The poor girl did not learn anything. She was completely ignored and became an outcast.

I walked to school every morning. On the way to and from school, I passed by an orphanage. It was a compound with high walls, the door was made out of steel with big locks, but one could look into the orphanage through openings in the wall.

In these openings, I saw many sad faces of small children, many were my age. I never saw them play but only standing around. There was one girl from the orphanage in our class. I never saw her smile or heard her talk or play with other children.

1957 Saigon Living at 128/15 Truong Minh Giang

What did the adults do to these kids? What would they be when they grew up?

When I finished fifth grade at Do Chieu School, I graduated from elementary school, it was my first step to go to high school. There were some good high schools for girls in Saigon during those years. Two of them were Gia Long High school and Trung Vuong High school. But I did not get accepted to those school. Acceptance to these Public high schools was very competitive and I was only eleven or twelve years old, and I did not know how to navigate my way to be accepted. For Profit schools were plentiful but the quality of education was very low due to big class sizes, the lack of teachers and lack of teaching equipment. The tuition students paid was not enough to cover those costs.

I think the year must have been 1957 or 1958. We had already moved to and settled at 128/15 Truong Minh Giang, Saigon. This is the year our mother gave birth to Hang.

Years of My Life

As I mentioned in a different chapter, at eleven or twelve years old, I was left on my own to manage my own academic experience. Overall, my middle school and high school years were much disorganized and fragmented. There was no guidance, little care from the adults and teachers.

Many school days, a few girls and I would not go to classes. Instead, we went to the park nearby and enjoyed ourselves. The park's name is Vuon Tao Dan, and this park was still there in 2020. I saw pictures of this park on the internet as well as when I drove by when I returned to Vietnam in 2017, and it had many trees and a lot of flowers.

Sometimes during these years, our mother took Hiep, Ty, Nga and Hang with her to Khanh Binh to be with our father.

In Saigon, Anh Tan, sister Khanh and I were left at home at 128/15 with Di Bay. I am not clear what Anh Tan and sister Khanh did and what school they attended.

1957 Saigon Living at 128/15 Truong Minh Giang

I remember sometimes I went down to Khanh Binh to visit our parents and the rest of the family. Khanh Binh is a small village on the Vietnam and Cambodian border. This side of the river is Vietnam, and the other side is Cambodia.

To get to Khanh Binh, one took a bus to Chau Doc, then crossed the river at Chau Doc, to the other side to catch a ride to Khanh Binh. The road to Khanh Binh was very rough and muddy with lots of potholes. The small bus and car ride was uncomfortable and crowded. It took four to five hours to get to where our father lived and worked. The total time from Saigon was about twelve to fourteen hours to travel from our home in Truong Minh Giang to get to Khanh Binh. That is when the weather and traffic were good,

In Khanh Binh, our parents lived in a house with a dirt floor. The house was not a comfortable place. It was constructed with primitive material. The thatch wall was made by mud, straw, and bamboo sticks. The roof was made by weaving and tying coconut leaves.

Years of My Life

Our parents did not have room for me in this house. School was nonexistent. Even a bad middle school like Tan Thanh school which I mentioned earlier.

The year must be 1959. Anh Tan was sixteen, Khanh was fourteen, Hien was twelve years old. Maybe we were 1 year older since the Vietnamese count their age different from what we do now.

We were lucky here; we lived in Truong Minh Giang until 1975 so it must have been seventeen years living in one place without having to move from one place to another.

1957 Saigon Living at 128/15 Truong Minh Giang

5

1958 My Fourth & Fifth grade at Do Chieu Elementary
September 24, 2022

It has been a while since I wrote about our family story. Today is Sept 24,2022 and autumn has just arrived. Leaves on the trees still green but pretty soon they will change color.

I believe we moved to 128/15 Truong Minh Giang in 1960 because that is close to my age at that time. I was in fourth grade of Do Chieu elementary school, a public school. The quality of education of public schools in Vietnam is completely opposite of quality of education of public schools in the US. To be admitted, even in grade school, to a public school in Vietnam one had to take an entrance exam.

The class sizes were small, students were selected and must be well behaved, obey the teachers and other adults. These are a few items I remember about my two years at Do Chieu school.

Here, I was allowed to go to school in the morning and sister Khanh in the afternoon. We had to share responsibly to help our mother in babysitting or some kind of housework. At school we learned the basic math, history, geography etc. nothing else, no music, no sport, no debate etc.

Now, we are very fortunate to have an opportunity to go to school and have a home to go back to. No matter how big or small that opportunity was, few girls had that opportunity.

I attended Do Chieu Elementary school and sister Khanh, Truong Binh Minh right outside our small alley to our back door at 128/15. Sister Khanh was not admitted to Do Chieu because she did not take the entrance exam.

1958 My Fourth & Fifth grade at Do Chieu Elementary

In fourth grade, Co Muoi was my teacher. She was about thirty-five to forty years old. Back then, teachers were allowed to whip students or to administer other kinds of physical punishment. Co Muoi did none of that to her students. Instead, when we did something 'wrong' she make us pay in money. The money was kept by an older student in class. At the end of the year, it was used to buy cloth. The cloth was then divided and shared with the class members.

Or another way of her punishment was to make the student write fifty to one hundred times the lesson that should have been memorized. Back then, memorization of your lessons was a big deal.

One thing she did that stands out vividly in my mind and which influenced me a great deal and which I still remember today was her method of punishment of my classmate, a girl name Nu, who was assigned a seat in the back of the class.

Nu was very quiet and did not stand out for some reason. Once she did not memorize her lesson, she was told to write it fifty times, but she failed to do that. The punishment doubled to one hundred times. She did not or could not do that.

Then her father, a cyclo driver, a person who pedals and use his physical strength to take customer to their destination, came to our class. The cyclo drivers earned very little money. In front of all students in the class, Nu's father yelled at Co Muoi. I remember loud voice exchanged between Co Muoi and Nu's father. After a while he left.

After that Co Muoi excluded Nu in all her teaching and class learning events.

For example, during math learning and practicing, all students were told to gather around the blackboard to solve a math problem as part of learning. She would tell Nu "Dear, you don't have to come to the black board, stay where you are and be comfortable." She treated Nu the same with all other learning and class activities.

1958 My Fourth & Fifth grade at Do Chieu Elementary

Back then, I did not understand the impact of being excluded from a group by a person who had undue influence.

I remember my fifth-grade teacher named Co Tu. She was younger than Co Muoi by a few years.

She spent a lot of time chatting with other teachers outside classroom on the hallway. Of course, when she was out chatting with other teachers, we class students would chat with our classmates. The class would get very noisy. Co Tu would come back to the class and use her ruler to slap our hands. All students were to line up and received this painful punishment.

Fifth grade slowly passed by. I finally graduated from elementary school. It was a benchmark of academic achievement.

Remember, our country was under the domination of the French for about one hundred years. During this time, the French wanted to keep all of us as dumb and as weak as they could. Because when you are dumb and weak, you accepted their domination.

Years of My Life

The French gave the Vietnamese Opium and alcohol and any other drug they can think of not to kill us because they still want to have a slave labor force.

After graduating from Do Chieu school, those lucky ones with parents or other adults helping, would know where to apply and take the entrance exam to attend a public high school. Our parents were away from Saigon. I did not know how and where to apply to get in the few public high schools in Saigon. I was left alone to determine my own future high school education.

I believe the first high school I tried out was Tan Thanh. Its classes were very, very crowded. There must be have been eighty to ninety students in a class. Of course, when a few teacher managed to get in the class to teach, he or she only taught the first two or three benches sitting in front.

Some of my classmates and I did not get a lot out of this school, so we usually left the classes and went to Tao Dan park to enjoy ourselves. No one cared if we lived or died. Our parents were not around.

1958 My Fourth & Fifth grade at Do Chieu Elementary

Our father and mother were in Khanh Binh at that time. Our father worked for the Vietnamese Government which was supported by the US. Our mother took Hiep and Thuy with her to live with him in Khanh Binh. Leaving our house and us to be cared for by Aunt Bay, our mother's younger sister.

At the end of that year, I must have been twelve or thirteen years old. Brother Tan attended Dong Tay Hoc Duong. So, our mother suggest that the rest of us should also go to that school.

At Dong Tay Hoc Duong I was in seventh grade. Classes were still crowded. Teachers could only teach the first two benches of students. Here I remembered sister Khanh was a favorite student of Mr. Hieu, the Vietnamese literature teacher. Sister Khanh was also a good friend of Kim Quy, who was from a fairly well-to-do family. Kim Quy had a birth defect; her leg was shorter than the other. They both were good friends and always stayed together. Somehow sister Khanh always had a knack of connecting with others.

Our math class teachers name was Mr. Bich. There was nothing special about him. However, one day, yes one day, in class he said something which I kept deep in my mind. Mr. Bich told another student in class this "You should never be afraid of spending money to buy a good book. A good book is the greatest investment one can make."

Perhaps, with other students, this statement was not even worth listening to, but not me.

Somehow, I listened, and it registered in my brain. "Ah, so I can buy books and learn more and be better." It was just like someone had given me a seed and told me that the seed would grow to be something wonderful.

A new high school, Le Quy Don, opened up near our house. The headmaster was a lady who advertised that she graduated from Duke University with a MA. Father said that we should go to that school so the headmaster can teach us. So, I attended Le Quy Don high school.

The school was less crowded than the previous two but in reality, the headmaster never knew who we were. Nor did she care.

1958 My Fourth & Fifth grade at Do Chieu Elementary

Here again, between sister Khanh and I we divided our time of going to school and helping our mother with babysitting and housework. The arrangement was that I went to school in the morning and stayed home in the afternoon and sister Khanh had the other shift.

In Vietnam at that time, students were required to take either English or French language class. I previously learned French but because I had the morning school shift and French was not taught in the morning and our parents allowed me to take English and catch-up classes in the evening. This was three times a week and two hours each, so students were supposed to catch up quickly.

Soon I think I had about a thousand English words in my vocabulary. In class we learned stories written in simple English such as *Hamlet* by William Shakespeare or *The Time Machine* by H.G. Wells.

I was fascinated with these stories and wanted to read more stories. Remember I told you earlier that books are not expenses but are investments. So, I wanted more books to read.

With the little money I had, I went to the bookstore Khai Tri in downtown Saigon and bought other stories also written in simple English. I bought and read *Jane Eyre*, and *Rebecca, Little Women.*

I admired and loved the heroes and heroines of the stories, so I kept on reading these books over and over. They are beautiful classic stories.

Vietnam literature also have many beautiful stories, I read many books by The Tu Luc Van Doan group. This is a group of Vietnamese writers that banded together and wrote beautiful novels with an ambition of changing the old Vietnamese thinking in terms of philosophy, family relationships, the concept of beauty and of life.

I stayed in Le Quy Don high school for two years; eighth and ninth grade. At the end of grade ninth grade all students had to take a three-day national exam to pass the Trung Hoc De Nhat Cap. This was the first High School Baccalaureate.

I passed this exam.

1958 My Fourth & Fifth grade at Do Chieu Elementary

6

1960-61 My Early Years

10/15/2023

Early this morning, just like any morning, This morning I rode my bike at the familiar trail at Grand Valley. It rained last night, the sweet aroma of the grass and the wildflowers freshly washed with rainwater raised up to my nose, and all of a sudden, my memory went back to the time we were in living in South Vietnam Mekong River Delta. Strange, how childhood influences stay with us the rest of our lives. Yes, it was there that I first smelled the freshness of rainwater that fell on wildflowers and grass after it rained.

Years of My Life

In a different chapter I will write about our lives in Rach Gia, then a small town in South Vietnam Mekong River Delta. For now, I will talk about my years in sixth and seventh grades. I was 12 years old.

Sister Khanh and Anh Tan were studying at Dong Tay Hoc Duong school. Anh Tan attended different classes than I.

Sister Khanh and I had some similar classes.

Sister Khanh had a close friend. Her name is Kim Quy.

They were often together, side by side. I think Kim Quy adored my sister Khanh. Kim Quy's two legs were not developed evenly so it caused her hardship in walking. Sister Khanh was always good at making friends with other girls. She and Kim Quy were always together, sometimes with other girls. Sister Khanh was also one of the favorite students of Mr. Hieu the Vietnamese literature teacher.

Our big brother Tan was attending the Dong Tay Hoc Duong school. Mother said we ought to come to the same school with him for him to watch after us if he is available.

1960-61 My Early Years

I do not remember seeing Anh Tan much but most of the time. I was in the same class as sister Khanh. She was my big sister and was always there for me.

At Dong Tay Hoc Duong, one day, one day. The math teacher, Mr. Bich, told the students his thought. He did not just talk to me, but to the whole class. Nobody paid attention but his message resonated with me and influenced me, for the better, for the rest of my life. The one sentence was, "You should never consider money spent on books as money spent, but as money invested with much return."

I will tell you later how this idea has influenced me.

I do not remember exactly how long I attended Dong Tay Hoc Duong Highschool. After that, our father was transferred to Nha Trang.

The year must be 1960-1961 because Thai was born, and our parents moved there. Hiep, Thuy, Hang and Ky and I went there. At first, I stayed at home and helped to baby sit as well as help our mother with household chores.

We lived in housing provided by the government. It was very plain, just a building without water or a bathroom. You had to go to the field behind the building or to the open beaches which are now gorgeous beach fronts for expensive hotels. How incredible is that?

I remember in my early teens I had to pull water from a well near the house to do the laundry. It was done by hand for the whole family. I also had to fetch water from that well to bring it to the makeshift kitchen for mother to use to cook and clean.

For daily food, our mother shopped at the local 'Chut' market near Cau Da. Farmers and fishermen sold their crops and fresh caught fishes there. Once a month she went to the Nha Trang Market to buy major items such as a big bag of rice and bottles of fish sauce etc.

1960-61 My Early Years

Our father worked in a government compound similar to the compound in Rach Gia. There was a chief who lived in extraordinary luxury with his family. I think this man was a widower, but he had two daughters. Later on, the older girl became sister Khanh's friend.

Here, Hiep and Thuy were good buddies, they had a great time when they went swimming, playing at a water hole filled with barbed wire and tadpoles. Many times, they brought home the tadpoles.

Hiep was also skillful at creating iguana traps out of bamboo to catch iguanas. Some of the iguanas were of fairly good size.

They often made kites from old newspapers and flew those kites high in the ocean wind.

As for me, I had a small doll without any clothing, so I managed to use some torn clothing to make a dress for my doll. This taught me the sewing skills which later on, I was able to use to make clothing for both Ron and I when we first got married and could not afford to buy clothes. We were very creative and made a lot of inventions from our humble sources.

One day on the beach, we witnessed and followed a man who raided the sea turtle nest and collected hundreds of sea turtle eggs. It was his price for catching and he kept the sea turtle eggs. I believe he kept the eggs and maybe he had sold or ate those precious eggs.

Hiep attended the elementary school nearby and our father homeschooled Thuy similar to how he helped Hiep a few years earlier. Mind you. Only boys received that attention. Girls, like me, never received such intensive coaching and tutoring. Ah, but I do not know if I would have liked that because our father was very strict. His words were the law.

As for me, I was happy to stay at home to babysit and help our mother with her chores.

But NO, one day, our father told me that I must go to school in Nha Trang for at least half a day each day. I was not happy with his decision, but no one can argue against our father, so I had to go to the Ngo Quy Don middle school in Nha Trang.

It is now a resort community with beautiful beaches in the center of Vietnam.

1960-61 My Early Years

For about 2 months, every afternoon I had to bike to school. It was a long bike ride along the road. On one side was the Vietnamese Navy compound, on the other side was the ocean. The ocean wind was strong, and I often had to bike against the wind. Additionally, the guards of the compound usually yelled some teasing and harassing words when they saw me, or any girls ride by. Oh, how I wished we had a little money so I could ride in the back of one of those public small Lambretta, three-wheel carriers.

At Le Quy Don school, the classes were crowded and noisy. I did not learn much but one day, I heard the boys in the class sing a song whose melody I really liked. A few years ago, I heard this song again on YouTube. I found out its name and author. It is the 'Do Chieu' song by Truc Phuong, the author. I still like the song to this day and was sad to hear of that the author's life in poverty and that he passed away destitute. In Vietnam, talented people are not treated well or maybe they did not know how to sophisticatedly develop their talents.

My study at Le Quy Don school in Nha Trang did not last long. It ended in about one and a half months to two. Because it was the end of the school year. Then, it was sister Khanh's turn to go to Nha Trang to live with our parents.

I was sent home by train together with a girl close to my age. I remember her name, Co Truc, who was the sister of our neighbor. It was arranged that way, so that in the adult mind, "two thirteen-fourteen years old girls could look out for each other." The train took the whole day to go from Nha Trang to Saigon.

It was here at Nha Trang that I learned how to speak with the Hue accent. Vietnam is a small

Country that had a distinct Northern, Central and Southern region. Each with a different accent. By the way you speak, they know what region you are from.

Central Vietnam is a poor area for agriculture because the land is full of sand and not fertile.

Vietnam geographically is in an S shape, the central is narrow, one side is mountainous.

1960-61 My Early Years

On the other side is the Pacific Ocean. Recently, the area became prosperous because of the beautiful scenery and gorgeous beaches.

At 12 years old, I was trusted with the awesome responsibility of managing my own education. No coaching, no advice, or teaching from adults. But I was lucky. I had a home to go back to and had food to eat, and parents who loved me even if they were not around.

My parents gave me some money to pay for school.

I was free to choose whatever school I wanted.

There were for profit schools. I think the owners were careless about the quality of education their school provided. They filled classes with students who probably did not know what to do or even to dream of a future.

I picked out a school named Tan Thanh because of its tall red brick building, and that its name was displayed on a huge billboard.

My classes were very crowded. They probably had eighty to one hundred students in each class. Students sat on benches that had a long table on which to write. Usually, it was very crowded.

If you were sitting in the middle of the class, you could not hear the teacher's lectures. The teacher could only teach one or two rows of students who sat in the front of the class.

Many days, I was very tired of listening to loud noises of students and could not absorb what the teacher said. A few girls and I would go to the Tao Dan Park to enjoy ourselves and not have to sit in those awful classes.

Tao Dan Park, then and now, is in the middle of Saigon. It is full of lush green, towering trees, and beautiful flowers. At the end of the day, I went home. Reporting to myself and my aunt who was there to help to feed us. As I remember that went on for a few months.

In the next chapter, I will talk about a different school when I was in grade eight. For now, I will tell you about how reading changed my thinking for the better.

My habit has always been that when someone says something that resonates with me, I will keep that advice. That advice then becomes my idea.

1960-61 My Early Years

My thinking has slowly changed because of what Mr. Bich said years ago about buying books being an investment. That idea went into the back of my brain where it stayed. Now I am looking for good books to read and good authors to admire.

I started out reading Vietnamese world class novels. by Khai Hung, Nhat Linh of the Tu Luc Van Doan Group. Their novels were very romantic. The characters are lovely, the stories are heart touching.

On my own, I studied more modern Vietnamese literature. I learned about authors who used their pens to encourage change of old customs and cultures. They wrote beautiful novels depicting love, sacrifice and the unfairness of society imposed on people who got caught in between the dawn of western influence and old Chinese obsolete influence. I read many novels of this group, the Tu Luc Van Doan, Self-Strengthening Literacy Group.

If you have not had a chance to read one of their books, you would not want to miss reading those. Perhaps by now they have the English Translation.

Vietnamese old customs and culture are for those with a narrow and harsh mind, but it influenced the whole Vietnamese society. It was especially harsh on women.

Though often on men too. They suffered different types of stress. There were double standards for men and women and also for different society classes. For example, the daughter-in-law is the 'property' of the husband's family, and she was often treated as such. This was especially true for the people in the countryside or those who tried to stick to the old way of thinking.

Khai Hung and Nhat Linh, through their novels, created characters that were trapped in those situations and society believed and sometimes that situation created tragedy. The situation could easily have been avoided had the characters' views been more open and accepting. Their novels also depicted love and sacrifice, the love of couples, parents, countries etc.

The new ideas and perceptions awakened in parts of my teenage brain. I started questioning the old Vietnamese customs and cultures and the old obsolete ideas imposed on us by the Chinese and then forcefully implemented by people in power who, then and now, want to preserve that power and pass it on to their children. The unfairness of the caste system was always imbedded in their minds but out of the corner of their mouth they always talked about "Their fellow brothers and sisters."

Years of My Life

1960-61 My Early Years

7

1961-1962 Returning to Saigon after Nha Trang

We finally arrived at Saigon from Nha Trang O Truc, O means Miss in Vietnamese, the neighbor's sister, and I she was greeted at the train station by her aunt and uncle. She came to live with them because her parents passed away in Hue. They were happy to see her. I then knew that my 'companion' responsibility was completed so I left and went home to Truong Minh Gang. Di Bay, our mother's youngest sister, was living with us while our parents were away. Di Bay had scoliosis since she was born. I remember our mother told us that when she was young and babysitting Di Bay, she felt a lump in Di Bay back.

Mother then told our Grand Mother about the lump but, of course, there was nothing our grandmother could do about this. Mother said Grandmother passed away very young, probably in her early thirty's, because of the 'Hau san Mon disease. Roughly translated, "slow dead after birth disease."

Di Bay did not marry. No one wanted to marry a woman with scoliosis. She did not receive any help from the government. The Vietnamese system was very bad for those with physical problems. No help, no social security, and no welfare. People had to depend on their relatives and their children. A lot of economic and support expectations were put on the sons of the family. The boys, therefore, were considered the 'family successor.' Thus, sons received a lot more attention and investments than daughters. They were the hope and the pride of the family.

Our father's job in Nha Trang ended after about a year or two. After that, he was transferred back to Saigon. So, mother, sister Khanh, Hiep, Thuy, Nga, Hang all returned with him. Our house was very crowded again.

1961-1962 Returning to Saigon after Nha Trang

It must be 1961. Our father worked in Saigon and Nga was registered to Do Chieu in Kindergarten/First grade. I remember many days, I had to pick her up from school with our father's 'Velo Solex.' This was a bike with a tiny machine attachment to its front wheel. It was tiny from today's perspective where we all drive a car with several hundred horsepower.

Every day he came back from work for a lunch break. He would hand over 'Velo Solex' to me and softly asked me to go to pick up Nga. Looking back this was of out of character for our father since he only gave 'orders.' Him asking was something I rarely witnessed or experienced.

Our father was a very good storyteller. Many women in the neighborhood loved to listen to his story. I remember he told us about the Dien Bien Phu battle in 1953 or earlier. This battle was the decisive battle for Vietnamese in the struggle for independence from the French. The Viet Minh defeated the French and won a big victory. The French suffered a major defeat. As a result, the Genève Treaty cut Vietnam into two regions, North Vietnam, and South Vietnam at the 17th parallel.

I did not clearly understand the details of the story he told us, but this intrigued me and made me want to know more about this battle and the history of Vietnam during this period. For years, I keep on wondering, what happened at Dien Bien Phu and how did it happen but either I did not have time or resources to investigate or the information available was so fragmented that it did not make sense. I found out more about this battle and some additional details about the battle and the defeat of the French in Ken Burn's recent documentary 'The Vietnam War.'

There was a new school in Phan Thanh Gian Street, Saigon. This one was named Le Quy Don. The owner and Headmaster was Mrs. Nguyen Ngoc Linh advertised her credentials of achieving an MA from some school in the US. Our father thought that it would be good for the girls to go to the school with the female Headmaster. He thought that maybe that would do us some good.

1961-1962 Returning to Saigon after Nha Trang

As always, Sister Khanh and I divided our time to attend school and stay home to help our mother with housework. Each of us would go to school half day and half day stay home to help. I was in eighth grade and my class was in the morning. The only foreign language offer in the morning was English.

All pupils, starting in the sixth grade were required to take either a French or English language course. In the sixth and seventh grade my foreign language was French. So, for me to enter the eighth grade and take English made it almost impossible for me to catch up without additional help.

Our parents agreed to let me study English in the evening, at a school offering special English classes. In those days, learning English in the evening was popular with adults since that could help them to get a better job with better pay.

The French dominated Vietnam for close to one hundred years. During this time, they suppressed education for the people because they did not want smart and educated local people.

The smart ones were hard to dominate and might overthrow their 'Lordship' position. In Vietnam dumb people did not know how to fight. The French created a situation that made it almost 'impossible' for a large number of Vietnamese to acquire an education.

I went to eighth and ninth grade at Le Quy Don High School and academically, I do not recall anything significant. I remember after I finished the ninth grade, I passed the 'First High School' exam referred to as Trung Hoc De Nhat Cap.

Boys with this degree could attend the Thu Duc Military Academy and would then become a Petty Officer. Thus, their time in the military might be better than the those that were privates.

In the English classes in the evening, we learned to read and construct some simple phrases, and stories. At first, our lessons were in one or two sentences and then gradually, we learned to read longer sentences, then paragraphs then easy stories. After a few months, we were able to read a simple story.

1961-1962 Returning to Saigon after Nha Trang

One story we read was "Little Women" By L.A. Alcott. It was written with simple English for beginners with only one-thousand-word vocabularies. From this story, I learned about the main characters, Josephine, Beth, and Amy. We also read a few pages of the great story 'Hamlet' by William Shakespeare. Again, it was in simple English for foreigners.

Finally, at a higher level, we read the fascinating futuristic novel *The Time Machine* by HG Wells. This is a great science fiction story and later on, it was made into a movie. It made such a big impression on me that I still remember the two species of humans of the future. They evolved into the Morlock and the Eloi. Reading this book encouraged me to read more. Reading opened a whole new horizon in my mind. The more I read, the more I enjoyed the stories, the places, and the characters.

Remember I told you about Mr. Bich who said that 'money spent on books was money well invested.' I went to Khai Tri bookstore in Saigon and bought some books with the pennies I had saved.

I found of all kinds of books in English which were written in simple terms for foreigners. I was not sure if I could read them, but I had always admired people who could read another language, I figured that I should at least try to read these. When I saw someone read a foreign language book or newspaper, I felt like I had to be able to do that. Buying an English book was an act of investment for me. I had hopes of achieving knowledge and enjoying reading.

So not knowing much what these books except that they were sold in a respectable bookstore, I trusted they were good books.

With very limited knowledge of English and budget, I bought and read, *Jane Eyre* by Charlotte Bronte, *Wuthering Height* by Emily Bronte, and *Rebecca* by DP Maurier. I must have read and re-read each of these English books several times. I had a dictionary in one hand and the book in another. The stories brought me joy and sadness. I admired Jane Eyre for her character and integrity.

1961-1962 Returning to Saigon after Nha Trang

Several years later, I found out that those books are world class literature. I still love the character, Jane Eyre. Jane is hardworking, romantic, courageous, passionate about life, loyal, honest, all the great qualities of a person.

Nowadays, I still tell members in my club that Jane Eyre is one of my favorite novels. To this day, I still seek out and watch this classic movie in black and white whenever they are available on TV. Those stories have so many twist and turns and the acting skills of the actors and actresses of the black and white movies are great.

The beginning of my dream of going to college in the US began in the small and muddy alley in the back of our house that was a short cut to Truong Minh Giang Street. On that street was a small newspaper and magazine stand that sold or rented papers and magazines.

One day, I picked up a magazine similar to the Reader's Digest Magazine and saw an article in Vietnamese, written by a Vietnamese author, who was a visiting professor at Berkeley, which was titled "He Berkeley" which means a summer at Berkeley University. That immediately caught my attention. I read the article and instantly the thought in my mind was, "Oh, How I wish someday I could go to a university like Berkeley. That was a dream, a wish that was probably harder to achieve than for many nowadays that want to travel to the moon for vacation. But it was the dream I kept in my heart and mind.

I remember in grade school, one day I had a geography lesson about the US, was reading it to memorize it. Our father heard my reading and commented "The US is the best country in the world." I really did not understand what he meant by that, but it resonated with me.

1961-1962 Returning to Saigon after Nha Trang

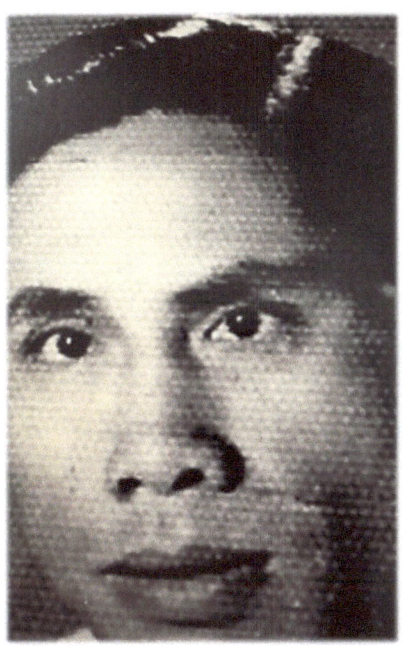

I often remember whatever another person says if the statement resonates with me. I keep that quote or statement for reference. In life, I have accumulated quite a bit of wisdom that others have said in person or have written in their books; from teachers, from friends, from co-workers and most recently from Dr. Steven Covey and his book *"The Seven Habits of Highly Effective People"* and also from my Yoga instructor and the Yoga Philosophy.

How could I expect to go overseas to study when my parents were still struggling with food and clothing for all of us? I had No money, no social prestige. Such a dream seemed so far out, so impossible.

Our parents had so many children and only one working man with ten to fifteen mouths to feed. One mother had to care for all of us. Our mother went to the hospital and brought home another baby every other year. We all loved the baby and were happy that both mom and baby were well but soon after that there was the bundle of work on all of us. Another baby, another bundle of work for me!!!

I did not have time to play with friends. All my available time was used to babysit younger brothers and sisters. If I accidentally drop the younger one when carrying them around, I would get punishment. I had often complained that our parents had too many babies and I really did not want to babysit that much. My childhood escaped me because of all the 'free' the time I had I have to babysit my younger siblings.

Whenever our father heard me complain about 'more babies' he would say 'having a lot of brothers and sisters is a blessing and not a burden. Oh, how could that be a 'blessing' I thought.

1961-1962 Returning to Saigon after Nha Trang

I had never had any attention from my parents. I never had time to play with my friends but plenty of time to babysit. I was not sure that I should listen to my father's teaching.

But I knew I could get away from that chores sometimes by telling my mother that "I had to do homework." So sometimes reading gave me a chance to escape babysitting. It was quite a great exchange.

Sister Khanh was much better at helping our mother with chores than I was. She worked and worked without complaining. She was a big help to Mother.

Growing up in Vietnam, physically, I had two things that most girls did not want. At five foot seven inches tall, 1.65 meter, I am too tall, and I had too thick and curly hair.. The double NO to the Vietnamese standard of beauty those days. I was often teased that I was "king-size" and that was devastating for a teenager.

It hurt and I had no one to turn to. Our parents would not have understood. Besides, they were too busy to listen to 'a kid's' story. Vietnamese did not praise their children to reinforce their self-confidence. They thought that praising their kids was unacceptable because the spirits might take that child away and that might not, please the 'neighbors' or 'relatives." We now all know that was a bad customs and belief.

I often went to the American library near our house and checked out books to read. More often than most, the books were too difficult for me to read but checking them out made me feel good. I thought that maybe, just maybe, one day, I could read them.

1961-1962 Returning to Saigon after Nha Trang

Years of My Life

8

1964-1966 The High School Years in Saigon

In 1964-1965 I passed the eighth grade which was the First High School Baccalaureate. It was a three-day comprehensive exam and a big accomplishment. The when the French controlled the Vietnam, they made the educational tests as hard as possible to keep the common people from achieving a higher education. They knew that educated people were more difficult to control. Passing this exam opened the door for me to go on to the next higher level.

With the First High School baccalaureate, if I were a boy, I would have been able to attend the Thu Duc Military Academy.

Upon graduation, I would have achieved the Chief Petty Officer rank and if I had to go to war, there would have been a little less chance of being shot at than the unranked soldier.

For grades nine, ten and eleven I moved to the Catholic High School, Le Bao Tinh High School, as mother suggested. Because Catholic priests ran this school there was more discipline in school and in classes.

Every morning before class we had to recite a pledge. I remember it went something like this: "Dear God, please help me to live nobly with much love to humanity, love and obey God. Amen (I don't remember the rest of the wording.) It is a very good pledge.

At Le Bao Tinh High School, in my modern literature class, we studied the works of recent authors. My favorite was the author of Tu Luc Van Doan, Khai Hung. I read many of his novels and was influenced by his ideas. I admired the heroes and heroines in their struggles to escape the slavery chains either mentally, physically, or both.

1964-1966 The High School Years in Saigon

While I am writing this, I checked Google for Khai Hung. There is so much more information than was available to students years earlier.

In my Vietnamese Literature classes, the author information was very incomplete and fragmented.

In Wikipedia, I learned a lot about Khanh Hung that I did not know. Best of all, I learned that for some part of his life he lived in Ninth Giang, Hai Duong province, which is where I was born. How cool is that?

At Le Bao Tinh High school, I excelled in both subjects of Math and English.

In English classes, I managed to keep two lessons ahead of my classmates. Yes, only two and that was all I needed to be considered 'very good.'

In math classes, I learned from a very well-known math teacher in Saigon at that time. Mr. Buu Huu Dot, who always told his students to keep all problems simple. I kept all my math problems simple, so it was very easy and clear. "Keep It Simple" is a timeless mantra.

At Le Bao Tinh High School, I had a good friend, Nguyen Thi Dung. We both loved to listen to music. Our idols at that time were Francois Hardy and Cliff Richard. We loved Francois Hardy singing but we "really" loved Cliff Richard's acting and singing. We watched the movies he starred in; "The Young Ones" and "Summer Holidays" over and over. To this day I love to listen to timeless songs sung by timeless voices.

I remember one day I was in Dung's house and listening to the songs; back then they only had the thirty-three rpm disks, or the forty-five rpm disks and I forgot what time it was. I was supposed to go home at dusk. Finally at ten PM I remembered I had to go home. As soon as I stepped inside the door, our father was waiting for me with his belt buckle in his hand and I received a whipping for staying out late. Wow. How scary was that.

Growing up in Vietnam for a young person it seemed that beating was the only way for adults to take their frustration out to the younger, smaller, and defenseless ones.

1964-1966 The High School Years in Saigon

That was not teaching, that was physical abuse but at that time it was the only way they knew how to do it. That was the only whipping I got from our father which I did not forget. I forgave him. It was the society he lived in and was part of. We all lived in that society.

Back to Vietnamese literature by Tu Luc Van Doan. I just googled the name Khanh Hung and saw a lot of information about him. I am amazed. I did not know any of this about the author, whose characters I love and admire. Khanh Hung had a lot of modern ideas. His idea of 'beauty' is different from that of the mass society. In nineteen forty-fifty for a man to be considered 'attractive' and 'desirable' he had to look frail, and very pale. He would have one-inch-long fingernails to show that he did not have to do any manual work. His clothing was a long dress similar to the Vietnamese women Ao Dai but his was usually black or white and worn over a trouser. Khanh Hung's idea of love and duty was not about obeying or yielding to higher authority and accept obsolete thinking but about having an open heart and open mind,

Author Khai Hung described a handsome man very differently. In one of his novels, he described the physical appearance of a character named Voi. Voi's skin was tan, a bronze tan. He had muscles and looked very strong, according to today's standard. Yes, this strong and good-looking man was not what people of the old way thought. They would have described him as an underclass laborer.

You should read Khanh Hung's novels. Make time to enjoy these masterpieces, just like I made time to enjoy the masterpieces of Victor Hugo's, *Les Miserable* or William Shakespeare's, *Hamlet*.

Khai Hung novels are about changing the obsolete Vietnamese customs and tradition. Those customs and traditions have done a lot of physical and mental damage to individual growth and thus society's growth. Individuals yearn to live a normal life as mother nature intended. He presented the heroine as the one who suffered the narrow mindedness of the society at that time.

1964-1966 The High School Years in Saigon

At the end of the eleventh grade, I passed another three-day comprehensive exam. Less than twenty percent usually passed this test. And many people retook the exam for many years trying to pass it. Some would be so disillusioned about failing it that they would commit suicide.

I passed the exam with flying colors. The only person in the family who recognized my achievement verbally was Uncle Be. He commented that, "Hien is the first girl in the family who achieved this level of higher education.

If a boy passed this exam, he would be eligible to attend the Da Lat Military Academy that was equivalent to the West Point Academy. Ah, but that was only a privilege for the boys. For a girl this was not possible, and it actually made it more difficult to get a date because many of the young men did not want to date a smart girl.

The eleventh grade was the highest and Le Bao Tinh high school. If one wanted to go on, they had to go to a different school.

I do not remember that I had a 'boyfriend' at that time. Growing up in Vietnam, I had two things that a girl did not want. I was too tall, five foot seven inches, and I had too much strong, black, and wavy hair.

A girl was considered beautiful if she were small; perhaps five foot or four-foot and some inches tall with very thin hair that would flow off her head as if she were in the wind.

I was often reminded by others that I am a tall, giant girl. Yes, that was devastating because most boys were only 5'3 or 5'4. I definitely did not want to go out or be seen with a boy who was a head shorter than I and no boy wanted to go out with a girl that was a head taller than him.

Ah, but looking back, I remember there was a classmate named Duc. Duc was taller than most boys. Probably my height. He usually rode his bike from his house in Go Vap to come up to see me at 128/15. But I paid no attention to him or anyone from Go Vap. After a while, he stopped coming. I did not know he was coming to see me.

1964-1966 The High School Years in Saigon

Hiep also attended Le Bao Tinh high school at that time. I remember one day our mother told me that I had to go talk to the Priest about Hiep on her behalf. Mother was always busy with little kids. Perhaps the high-powered priest 'intimidated her. He was the one who controlled students and walked the hallway in his black gown. The priest was not really that bad. I was a well-behaved young girl. Never got in any trouble with school authorities.

So, I went and talked to the Priest, but he dismissed me saying that "You and your brother collaborated with each other, I need to talk to your mother.

I don't remember where my sister Khanh went to high school during those years.

I remember Anh Tan was in big trouble with our father when he was 15 or 16 or 17 years old, that means I was 11 or 12 or 13 years old.

One day at our home on 128/15, Chi Tam, who used to work for our mother as a helper, came to our house and told our parents that Anh Tan was at her house with his pregnant girlfriend. Anh Tan was seventeen and I think the girl was eighteen.

This girlfriend's name is Duyen. She is the mother of the five kids he had with her; Phuong, Diem, Toan, Cu Lon his nickname, I remember his real name is Khoa Nguyen.

Our parents, of course, arranged the wedding. Duyen's mother expressed her appreciation to our parents for having lifted the shame their daughter created for them.

Back then, you brought shame to your family if you were in love with someone. How sad. It was, however, the thinking of the time. It was ok for the boy to have many girlfriends but not so for the girl, who was just allowed one boyfriend. Similar to the US nowadays, it is ok for the male to impregnate a woman but then too bad, she has to carry the child, no matter what.

1964-1966 The High School Years in Saigon

Years of My Life

9

1966 In the Beginning, A Miracle.

I believe in miracles.

Miracles many times arrive as a very difficult situation. I believe God wants to test us to make sure we are capable of handling the situation and worthy of the blessing he gives. So, take a deep breath and read through these pages. I will tell you about the time I was an unwed mother and the birth of Thu.

There was a young man who lived near our home at that time. He was tall, handsome, quiet, polite, and always well dressed. He played the violin. I was impressed by his manners and appearance. I did not know where he came from or what his background was, but I know I had a special feeling for this man.

A long, long time later, I think I found out what his name. I think it is Phan Boi Hoan, but I am still not sure. He was perhaps five years older than me. I was seventeen and he must have been twenty-four or twenty-five at that time.

I heard the neighbor say he came from the South Vietnam delta. He was probably from a well to do family. He came to Saigon to study and avoid being drafted to the war. Of course, who wanted to be killed in the American tragic war of the sixties.

We subsequently dated. We met a few times for the movies, for a walk. He still did not say much about himself, but I did not worry about his background, or who he was, or where he came from. Those things were not important to me. I just knew that I was happy to be with Hoan. We had a good time when we were together. That was all.

We dated for a while, for me, it was purely a romance. Later I found out I was pregnant. To this day of the Fall of 2022, I still don't know how it happened, and I am content and happy with thinking that it was a miracle, and it was God's will.

1966 In the Beginning, A Miracle.

Fifty-six years later, I still believe in that thought. Many times, God tested people before bestowing a miracle.

Time has proven that my feeling is right. Miracles many times disguise as challenges, and difficulties.

Thu is a beautiful woman, a daughter, wife, and mother now. She is successful and has a wonderful family that is God's blessing.

With her arrival I worked hard, finding all the ways I could to get out of the situation in we were in, in Vietnam. I succeeded; we all are all now living happily in America, our beloved country.

Right after I found out that I was pregnant I immediately cut off our relationship.

I did not let Hoan know. Even at seventeen, my pride was immense. For me to ask anyone for help or disclose my vulnerability was out of the question.

I told myself that I would handle the situation myself. No one would tell me what to do. I was determined to handle the situation myself.

First, I had to be financially independent. I could depend on my parents to support me or my child.

This was the most difficult period of my life. I was confused, bewildered, and worried. I was seventeen years old. Society was then and probably still is very harsh on unwed teenage mothers.

I set out to find a job. The job I found was as a clerk for the US First Infantry Division located in Di An, just outside Thu Duc province.

The pay was thirty-two UN dong an hour which at the time that was equivalent to US thirty-five cents an hour.

To get to work every day, I had to catch a fifty-five to seventy minutes Lambretta ride from Duong Hai Ba Trung street in Saigon near Ben Bach Dang to a location near Thu Duc market where a US military bus was waiting to pick us up. The Lambretta was a three-wheel small carrier.

Every day, the dark brown US military bus picked us up and drove us another hour to an hour and a half to Di An. The road was baked with red dirt and filled with potholes everywhere and when the wind blew, red dirt flew high.

1966 In the Beginning, A Miracle.

It stuck to our hair, permeated to our skins and clothing. It changed everything to the dark red dirty looking color.

After a more than one hour riding, we finally would arrive at Di An and the US First Infantry military compound was inside the area called the Iron Triangle.

Before we could go inside the gate, we had to get out of the bus and go through security and MP checkpoint. At the checkpoint, our body was searched and touched. Women by a woman guard and men, by a male guard.

Our personal belongings were also subjected to search and inspection by US Military Police. Once, I saw the MP pushed his hand knife through a person's meal container. I think he wanted to make sure that there were no weapons hidden inside the container. I was deeply offended but kept the feeling to myself.

Food, to me, was precious and not to be 'invaded' with filthy acts such as this one. But I had no way out. I just bend my head and looked the other way.

Years of My Life

My working day at First Infantry Division was very harsh. We, the workers, usually arrived at the working tents at around 10 AM. These were military tents which were set up in the middle of the jungle in this harsh Iron Triangle area.

No air conditioning, and no running water. Every day we did our work which was manual filling of the stock cards into files. These cards are similar to the IBM cards back in the old days when computers could only read the cards.

The days were harsh, hot, and long. Not so much the work but the conditions we had to work in were.

At 4pm the military bus came and picked us up and drove us back to Thu Duc Market. This was the reversal of what we had to done in the morning. At Thu Duc market, I had to find my way home back to Saigon.

I usually got back to Saigon around 6 or 6.30 PM.

It was a twelve-hour-a-day job. An exhausting trip with meager pay for only 8 hours work each day.

I usually wore a Vietnamese white ao dai. At the beginning of the day, it was white but at the end of the day it turned red because of the red dirt in Di An.

1966 In the Beginning, A Miracle.

Many days, our drivers were drunk. There were two American soldiers one driving the bus, the other guarding us. They hid their bottles inside a brown paper bag and drank while they drove us. They probably wondered 'What am I doing here? I am sure they were thinking about the that they were there because of the ambition of crooked politicians and corrupt big business.

Father was disappointed in me and my new job as a clerk. He wanted me to quit because 'girls working for the Americans were not well regarded in Vietnam at that time.

My work every day was just like that. It lasted until I was 7 months pregnant, and my stomach began to show.

Then one day Mother noticed my physical condition because of my growing belly. She confronted me and asked me if I was pregnant. I said yes.

Quietly and slowly, she said in this house, there was Khanh and now there are two of you. I told her not to worry because I would go away.

I had saved my money while I was working. I bought an airplane ticket to Hue where my friend Dung was stationed. Dung finished high school and decided that she would join the military. She became a Vietnamese Sergeant. Her main job was as an interpreter for high-ranking US military personnel.

Dung and four other girls lived in an empty, old Vila in Hue. This was their government housing.

The girls name and ages are: Chi Hung, she was the oldest at twenty-two, Hoi, was seventeen or eighteen and vulnerable just like the rest of us. Another girl, I don't remember her name let's call her Huon, was also seventeen or eighteen. She appeared to be more mature than Hoi or me.

Dung gave me her cot to sleep on. All the girls slept in their own simple military camping cot. Dung found herself in a different corner of the house where she slept. How sweet and generous of her.

1966 In the Beginning, A Miracle.

I just stayed there as a seventh- and eighth-month pregnant teenager. Not knowing enough or thought important or necessary to tell my friend or her co-worker and roommates why I was there. How ignorant and gullible I was.

Hue is an Old Imperial city thus the custom and culture was very harsh especial to women and particularly harsh to pregnant and unwed teenagers. I was not even aware of this.

Morning workday for my friend Dung and other girls began when a military driver and jeep came to the house and picked them up. The girls wore military uniforms and to me they looked strong and beautiful.

I stayed back in the house by myself and took a lot of walks to the market or the surrounding area.

I received Father's letter while in Hue. He said I brought shame to my family, and I should keep going.

I also received Mother's letter. She said she felt very sad and worried for me and that I should come home if I thought I should.

Nowadays, Oct 2022, looking back I think I understand my parents' feelings at that time. They were the product of the society at that time.

In Hue, it was never in my mind to find out where the hospital where I would deliver my baby or find out who would deliver my child or where I will be when the baby came. I did not think of or even knew how to handle anything. Looking back, I was completely oblivious to reality and what would happen in a month when the baby was due.

That time came. One night, probably around 4 AM in the morning, I felt a long and hard cramp in my stomach and could not sleep any more. I woke up.

Chi Hung was also up. She immediately recognized my situation and said the baby is coming, let's call a jeep from the military compound across the street to take her to the hospital.

A few minutes later, the military driver with the jeep showed up. The driver asked my friend 'Where will I take her?'

"I don't know where," was her response. Just take us to a hospital. Any hospital or midwife house will do.

1966 In the Beginning, A Miracle.

The driver said 'How about I take her to the hospital where I took my wife when she was expecting a child?

That sounded great to me.

On the way to the hospital, we passed through Hue's famous bridge Truong Tien, I remember the morning was clear and when I looked up, I saw the beautiful sky which was full of bright stars and a gorgeous looking clear moon.

How about I call my child Truong Thu? I had thought of the name Thu before. Perhaps Diem Thu but Truong Thu seemed better.

We arrived at the baby delivery facility. I did not know the content of the conversation exchanged between my friend Dung, the driver, and the head nurse. I was in too much pain to listen.

I remember the head nurse tried to deliver the baby, but she had some problem.

The nurse said she had to call the Doctor. So, I was laying there in bed and waiting for the doctor. It was so painful that I got mad when the doctor did not come sooner.

Finally, the doctor came and within a few minutes he delivered Thu. She came out as a healthy and strong little baby. Her crying was loud and clear. I felt so physically light that I thought if I spread my arms out and could fly.

Thu was born on September 29, 1966 in Hue. I stayed in this town with my friend Dung and her other roommates for a month.

After months of carrying a baby, now without the weight of the baby, water, and placenta I just lost several kilos of weight. I could go home now. Without a pregnant belly, my parents would not have to be ashamed of me.

After Thu was born, I had to stay in the midwife compound for another week under the nurse's observation. Here, I had to hire a helper and give her the money to buy my food and Thu's formula. The arrangement was completely different from the hospital in Saigon where our Mother gave birth to my younger brothers and sisters as I remembered.

1966 In the Beginning, A Miracle.

My helper is was an older woman. She had experience in helping women's birthing time. She bought red rice and cooked it for me. She said red rice would help me to recover more quickly.

After staying at this Midwife facility for a week, I left and went back to the house where Dung and the girls lived. This time, with a baby. I remember Thu was a very good roommate. She did not cry or wake up at night, so the rest of my roommates seemed to accept her well. Dung's helper, O Tam, helped by fixing up formulas and washing the cloth diapers.

I don't remember if I paid O Tam anything. Maybe I did, maybe I did not.

After I stayed there one month, I gave Dung money and asked her to get me an airplane ticket to fly back to Saigon with Thu.

Due to bad weather in the fall in Hue the airplane was rescheduled several times. Finally, it flew to Saigon.

I remember the day I left Hue and rode in a Cyclo to the airport with the baby in my arms. Walking up to my seat inside the airplane, I felt like a free person. My parents wouldn't have to be shameful because of my pregnancy. I had solved the shame they were very much afraid of.

When the airplane landed in Saigon, I carried Thu in my arms and walked to the bus which would take us to the passenger station near downtown Saigon.

I saw Mother and sister Khanh waiting for us when Thu and I arrived at the station.

Sister Khanh took Thu to Co Them's house for her to take care of and our Mother took me home at 128/15. Mother brought me home. Ah, my stomach was a lot smaller now. No one can say that I have an unwed baby. That was in my thinking.

Another chapter of my life had now begun.

1966 In the Beginning, A Miracle.

10

1967-1971 Working for the USA

I immediately looked for work. I knew that I must have income to pay for Co Them to take care of Thu and me to pay and help my mother.

I found a job with the Symantec Corporation as part of an interview team. I understand this company was doing research in Vietnam similar to the Rand Corporation's work. My team went to the field, areas where the RVN Government had just reoccupied after fighting with the VC, to interview local people about their thinking, past, present and wishes for the future.

We each carried a dozen or so drawings with no descriptions, we asked the local what they saw, what they thought about, what lead to the situation and their wishes.

We travelled to many areas far away from the big cities, it was dangerous. Nowadays, looking back, I realize I could have lost my life, lost my freedom and how dangerous it was if my team and I were captured by the enemy.

1967-1971 Working for the USA

There were times when our team would fly to the remote areas for the data collection task. The Pilots were usually American. They used the Cessna 1 engine to transport us from one place to another.

We would interview the locals, recorded their responses, then bring the answers back to the office to be translated into English. I think the results then were sent to the Department of Defense.

Back then, I was oblivious of the dangerous situation of the war. I was just focused on earning money. I had to have an income; this was an absolute requirement.

I do not think my mother knew enough to care for my safety. My father was working in Khanh Binh.

Earning a living was most important.

The project lasted for few months. When it was over, all of us were laid off. No additional compensation, no thank you, nothing.

Years of My Life

After several small jobs with US military, not long after that I found another job with the US Navy group called Personal Response Office. This group was led by a Chaplain. Its Purpose was to create understanding for the US Naval Personnel in Vietnam to understand more about the local customs and cultures.

To win the war in VN, the US advocated that their soldiers should learn to understand the Vietnamese, its customs, and cultures. The idea was noble; the intention may have been 'good.' We all know the results of the war. I am not going to discuss the politics here.

I want to share with you my years of working for the Chaplain's office, my office mates, the US Military personnel, our office mates, and my work

There were five Vietnamese in our office. Three of them were office workers only Kim Cuc and I were field assistants. Our duties when we are in Saigon included giving a tour of Saigon for the newly arrived US Naval Personnel. Answer the questions they had about the Vietnam and the people.

1967-1971 Working for the USA

We also travelled to the country side with the Chaplain and other team officers. We visited different Naval bases throughout South Vietnam. Naval bases

usually were in safer areas compared to the Marine or Army bases.

Kim Cuc and I taught easy Vietnamese languages classes to US Naval personnel. Speaking a little Vietnamese was one way to earn peoples good will. This was the most fun and interesting job Kim Cuc, and I had.

We were playing the roles of a peace makers. We travelled to the country side to with Navy Doctors or Corpsman to give medical care to local people. Here are few pictures which I save. I was an interpreter for the team.

Many Saturdays mornings, I rode in a gun ship helicopter with a group of Navy Doctors, Dentists, Nurses to fly to the neighboring war zone near Saigon, Nha Be to treat the local people who came to our team for treatment.

1967-1971 Working for the USA

While riding the Helicopter, I used to sit in the middle seat. On my sides are two helicopter gunship personnel. Just like you would see in a movie, their huge machine guns were pointed to the ground, tons of ammunition are placed nearby. Fortunately, with God's Blessing, on my trips, I was not in a gun fighting battle.

Our medical team usually returned to Saigon base in early afternoon.

Not all of my adventure with the Navy was war related. Once we rode a helicopter from Saigon to the VN Delta to attend the wedding of one of our team members. He married the American military nurse he met in Vietnam.

I remember LT O'Brian; we called him Anh Ba. Anh Ba is thin and tall. He was a good-natured man.

Remember I told you that as a Vietnamese girl growing up in Vietnam, I am 1.65 meter which is way too tall to considered a beautiful girl. Strange isn't it? On top of that, I have very thick and curly hair. Another negative for a girl.

One day in a casual conversation with Anh Ba, I told him that I am not a good-looking Vietnamese girl because I am too tall and have too much hair. In an astonishment voice, Anh Ba said," No Co Hien, look, you are a very beautiful girl. You are as beautiful as my wife. Don't listen to them. Do you know what a not good-looking girl looks like? There, you see. Look at those big and floppy nurses over there. Then in half joking voice, he added, we sent them over here in a project to beautify America. Ah, so then I got it.

1967-1971 Working for the USA

For years, I was always conscientious of my height, I was teased many times about this 'awful' factor. I was now surrounded by US Navy people; they are all taller than I am. I liked to mingle with a group of people who do not call me 'giant' or 'king size.'

Kim Cuc and I had very good time working for the US Navy. Not only was our pay much better than the local pay. We could also travel with Chaplain and his team all over Vietnam war zone. We were oblivious to the danger of the war. We did not think that the enemy could touch us. Nowadays, as I look back, I realized how clueless we were.

The war subsequently died down. In the US, war protesters were all over the country, from University Campus to Washington DC and many other towns. For a long time, both Kim Cuc and I realized that we could not stay in Vietnam when the Communist took over South Vietnam. We must get out.

I started to apply for College in the US. A US student visa would get me out of Vietnam, the process for me to get a Vietnamese passport and the US visa is worthy of a book by itself.

November 1971, I left Vietnam for the US. January 1972 I started at Pensacola Jr. College as a freshman. The war in Vietnam ended few years after that with the victory of communist North Vietnam.

April 1975 is the destiny time, 19 years. My father moved us from the North to the South VN in 1954. In1975 the Communist won.

1967-1971 Working for the USA

Years of My Life

11

1971-1975 The College Years

Today is 12-29-2023. Hien and Ron's 50th wedding anniversary.

I had a dream of going to college in America since I was a small girl. I remember one day at home at 128/15 when I was reading aloud a geography lesson about the US, and father commented that the 'US was the best country in the world.

That comment resonated with me. I thought to myself, "when I grow up, I would like to go there just to see what it looks like." It was the start of a dream, a dream that at that time was indeed far away, too untouchable. Our family was not rich, and I could not see how that could happen. One father worked to feed the whole family of ten or more people.

Yet, that was my dream.

The years went on.

I loved to read. One day I noticed the Thoi Nay, a periodical like Reader's Digest, at the newspaper magazine stand located on Truong Minh Giang Street just outside the little muddy alley leading up to the back door of our home. I read the magazine and noticed an article which was written by a Vietnamese in the US with the title "Summer in Berkeley."

I did not know who the author was nor, exactly where Berkeley was. But from reading the article, I found out that it is a college in California. Another flickering of light lit up inside my head. Yes, if this Vietnamese professor can be there, so maybe I could too.

The dream of going to college in the US grew bigger and bigger in me. I cherished the thought. In my mind I envisioned that I was walking across the university campus in the middle of tall trees and green grass with books in my arms.

Life went on.

I often went to the US library in Saigon and checked out books that listed the name and address of the US universities. I took the test of English as a second language as required by the universities. I then wrote letters to the universities and asked them for their catalog and application.

1971-1975 The College Years

To my happy surprise, the universities sent me their application and catalog. All the colleges required a $25 college application fee. I did not have the $25 to pay the fee so I sent in my applications without the payment.

To my pleasant surprise. I was accepted to some colleges.

Getting a visa to get out of Vietnam during the height of the war was very difficult and almost impossible. First because the Vietnamese government was restricting the flow of the Vietnamese people and money out of Vietnam. Second, all the big named politicians and business people kept a few visa spots available for their own children.

But "a dream is a dream, is a dream to accomplish." Relentlessly I kept on trying and trying.

I succeeded.

In November of 1971, I arrived in the US to go to college with an F-1 Visa.

From 1971-1973 I attended Pensacola Jr. College. These years were the most beautiful and remarkable years of my life. Not only did I achieve my dream of going to college in the US to earn a western education and knowledge, but I also achieved many dreams that I could not have imagined.

Years of My Life

At Pensacola Jr. College, I met Ron, I made many good friends, learned from inspiring teachers, studied western history and the arts, learned skills which later became invaluable in life. Most importantly I got a job that gave me the ability to sponsor my family into the US after the fall of South Vietnam.

At Pensacola Jr. College, my most impressionable teacher was Dr. Carageorge who taught Western Civilization History. I loved to come to his class and listened to him talk about western civilization from the beginning to present time. Most of the time, I understood the lecture but sometimes I did not due to the language's differences between Vietnamese vs English. At midterm exam I ended up with a very low grade. Dr. Carageorge called me to his office and told me that the score was the result of the language difference and not my abilities or desire. He then assigned a senior to be my tutor to work with me. He allowed me to retake the exam and replaced the score with the much better new score that I earned after getting tutored.

At the end of that semester, I brought him a Camelia flower from my front yard.

To this day 2023 I still remember him.

I had another memorable teacher. Mr. Seiler, a botany teacher, who inspired me to love and respect plants. I remember he stood in front of the class and with conviction, he told the students about the struggle for the survival of plants. Yes, nowadays, I still remember his image and lectures. The knowledge I learned from his class is still in me now and into the future.

Of course, I excelled in all my math classes. After one math exam, Mr. Barbee, the math teacher, announced "the grades in this class range from zero to one hundred." Guess who is the student received the perfect math score in an American math class, which was taught in English.

It was me.

I also loved classes such as Philosophy, Art, and Music. I would not have earned that knowledge if I had been in Vietnam.

On the extra curriculum side, I was elected as the president of the PJC Diplomats Club. It was a club for international students in this tiny community college, tucked away in the deep South. I also received a $500 Leadership Scholarship award and had a picture taken with the college President and other club presidents

Five hundred dollars was more than enough to pay for one year of tuition.

Louisa Peyton was a remarkable friend I met at PJC. Louise is blind. I heard that she was born prematurely in Europe during the war. She was placed in an incubator due to some insufficiency of the medical condition causing her to lose her eye sight. I believe she gained a sixth sense due this loss. She was smart, fun, witty and very much in love with life. I never heard her complain about not being able to see.

On many Friday evenings, we went to the movies together. While watching the movie she would explain to me the major points of the story. Occasionally she would ask me a question such as, "What is the color of her dress?"

"Purple, I would whisper" and my questions were, "what does he/she mean?"

Every school morning, I came to her house which was close to my apartment to pick her up for school. This saved her mother from having to drive her.

Jim and Lis Patrick were also some very good friends. We often studied together in their apartment near PJC. I understand they met in Germany where Jim was stationed as a member of the US military. Jim and Liz were both grade A students at the college. They are about 8 and 10 years older than me.

One day, yes, one day at one of my final exams, a friend Carol and I took the exam together. Carol finished first. She then turned to me and told me that, "There is a guy who wants to take you to dinner, and I told him that I would introduce you to him, so I will wait for you to finish your exam."

1971-1975 The College Years

I told Carol, "Oh no, go ahead and go home to be with your kids, it will take me a while longer."

Carol said, "No, I'll wait."

When the final exam was over, Carol and I walked to the Student Center. There I met a man who looked like a 1960's leftover hippy. His hair and beard were long and untidy. He wore a big brown patterned T-shirt with sleeves that had miss matched lengths and pattern. His cutoff shorts were ragged and torn. His toes were sticking out from open sandals.

Carol introduced him, "this is Ron a friend that I have at PJC." After the casual introduction Carol left.

Ron offered to buy me a coffee but after digging in his pockets, he did not even have twenty-five cents. He claimed he had left his wallet at home. I bought the coffee for both of us.

Ron told me that he was living with his parents.

I wondered, "If he was going to tell me a story." He looked old and ragged. During our conversation, Ron invited me to go sailing in his brother's sailboat. I always liked the water, so I accepted.

Ah, on the day we went sailing, I saw his brother's sail boat. It was a tiny Styrofoam boat. But I got in the boat anyway. The date went ok.

He was a nice person, so we dated a few more times. Nothing was impressive.

I continue to study with Liz and Jim my German friends at their apartment. One day, yes. That one day again. Liz asked me, "Hien you have been dating this guy Ron for 6 months now. How is he?"

I replied, "He seems to be nice, but I don't know."

"Why do you say that" Liz asked?

"I don't like the way he dresses. I don't like the way he looks."

Liz, then, said "Oh, those are the things you can change."

A big light bulb lit up in my brain. I had not had that thought. I did not know that I still needed a mother. From that day on, I saw Ron differently.

On one rainy morning, near the semester final exam time. While we were sharing an umbrella and walking across PJC campus together, Ron commented, "That it was a beautiful day. Do you think what I am thinking of on a beautiful day like this one?"

I thought, "here again, some more dry humor." I replied, "No, what are you thinking of."

Ron said, "I think we should get married."

I quickly replied to this humor, "Why not." Right after saying that, I realized Ron was serious.

That was his marriage proposal, and I had accepted.

Destiny comes at the least expected moment.

Shortly after, we got married on December 29, 1973.

It was our fifty-year wedding celebration in 2023.

1971-1975 The College Years

We both graduated from PJC at the end of that semester. After that, we moved to USF in Tampa to finish our education.

I had exactly thirty days in Pensacola to prepare for our wedding, finish the final exams, and pack up and move to Tampa.

It took us eighteen to twenty-four hours to move from Pensacola to Tampa. This is usually an eight-hour drive.

The reason it took so long was that we were driving an old one-ton step van which Ron bought to make his tool shed to build the boat with which he had planned to sail around the world. He still has the blue print of that boat. The towed vehicle was an old broken down barely road worthy 1960 Mercedes which he said he paid three hundred dollars.

While we were moving on the road at lower than the allowable speed, Ron's van threw the retread on his front tire and his tow bar pulling the old Mercedez that, he had made from some pipes, crumpled.

Conrad, his brother, was also traveling with us because he wanted to move to Tampa ended up driving the Mercedez and followed behind us.

We stopped on the road several times from early dawn into midnight. Ron would pull over and get both Conrad and I out of our cars and make us do jumping jacks with him so we could all stay awake.

Finally, around three or four in the morning of the next day, we pulled into our trailer park just outside USF. The address I remember is Box 1, Route 460, lot twenty-three, Thonotosassa, Florida.

It was our home until Ron graduated with a master's degree in mechanical engineering in December 1977.

1971-1975 The College Years

I graduated from USF in June 1975. It was about 3.5 years after I arrived in the US. I did not have much time in college. Always in the back of my mind was the need to hurry up, get out of school, earn money, to send home to my family who desperately needed it to survive and to support both of us while Ron was still in school.

Our years at USF were full of significant and personal events.

First, back in Vietnam my mother was getting sicker and sicker. Despite her condition, she continued struggling to make sure the kids had food to eat.

Second, Father was forced into retirement because of his age, I think 55 or 60 years old. He had yet another family with kids to support. I did not know this fact, or I did not allow myself to know.

As a poor struggling student at USF, I continued to send money to Vietnam. Many months the amount was only $50.00 but I always make sure I sent something.

To earn income, Ron and I opened a moving and hauling business, using his one-ton step van. We charged twenty dollars a load. Ron would pick up the trash, yard waste, and take it to the dump. He also hauled odds and ends for people. I advertised the business in the local newspaper and made appointments. The business survived for a short time, then one day, an official government letter came in the mail informing us that we were running the business without proper license and must stop or else.

So, we then had no business.

Our home was a humble twelve by forty-four-foot trailer that was parked in the middle of an abandoned orange field in a town named Thonotosassa, just a few miles from USF. We had all the oranges we could eat. The old frost damaged orange trees, despite their poor condition still struggled to produce but the oranges had great flavor.

Ah, trees are just like people. They have the same desire. To survive and to pass on their genes.

I spent one and a half years at USF with the intention of graduating as fast as I could. Then my goals were to find a job and earn money to send to Vietnam to help my mother feed my younger siblings and Thu. I had no time for student activities such as clubs, sororities, or partying. One and a half years to finish what a normal student would spend two and a half years doing.

It cost eight dollars to get into Bush Garden, a beautiful theme park nearby, but I did not have the money or the time to spend half of a day to be at the park.

Ron's and my Friday night outing was to do our laundry at a nearby laundry mat and do grocery shopping.

Our income included Ron's $300.00 a month of GI bill allowance. I had a student job at the computer room input/output window, earning a minimum wage of $2.75 per hour. Ron also co-opted at the Tampa Electric Company.

1971-1975 The College Years

Ah, but think about it. Gas was around forty cents a gallon. With my hourly salary, I could fill up my VW gas tank.

How many working people can make that claim in 2023?

June 1975, I graduated from USF with an Accounting degree. Job openings were scarce; especially for a fresh graduate without any "work experience."

I finally landed a job as an assistant auditor for Blue Cross of Florida. My pay improved significantly. My salary was $10,000 a year or $384 a week. I got paid every two weeks and alternately send one check to Vietnam to my brothers and sisters, and another other check was used for our living expenses.

Ron stopped co-opting for Tampa Electric and concentrated on finishing his master's degree at USF.

After Ron successfully finished his education, Ron was employed by the Procter and Gamble Company as an engineer.

December 1977, I resigned from my job as a Medicare auditor for Blue Cross of Florida. We moved to Cincinnati, Ohio.

Ohio has been our home and sweet home since then. Kurt was born on November 25, 1981, and Derek, November 19, 1987. Our children Thu, Kurt, Derek are successful and happy.

Today, July 22, 2024, as I sit in my comfortable office at my beautiful home in Indian Hill, Ohio, and I think back to my college days I am grateful I had the opportunity to study and to meet the wonderful people I met.

All my brothers and sisters are now US citizens, they are educated, have stable income, and a happy family life.

How I wish our parents were still with us to witness the success of their children.

1971-1975 The College Years

12

1975 and the Following Years to 1982

The year 1975 is one of the most significant years in Vietnam history. That year I was a senior at the University of South Florida (USF), Tampa. I was looking forward to graduating with an accounting degree. I hoped to find a good job with good pay so I could help my family in Vietnam more.

Mother had always expressed her expectation of her children's helping the family. I understood that and had been doing as much as I could in previous years and was happy to do more in the following years.

Ron and I had been married for more than a year. We lived in a small trailer in the middle of the abandoned orange field in the Thonotosassa area located just a few miles from USF.

Then in April 1975, two months prior to my graduation, South Vietnam collapsed. The victorious North Vietnam were now the rulers. I was devastated. That meant that I lost my family in Vietnam. I blamed myself for going to college and preparing for 'the peace time' and not 'the war time.'

What was I to do with a degree and the money I would earn? How would I help my family, my mother, my father, my brothers, and sisters?

I saw on TV that the US evacuated many Vietnamese refugees, and I had a thin hope that some of my family members would be in that group.

That year and the following few years were some of the most difficult years for my family in Vietnam. I will do my best to write down what I remember. Tragedy happens and we want to forget about it to move on with life.

1975 and the Following Years to 1982

The new Vietnamese regime took over. Father lost his job, lost his pension after more than thirty years of service with the South Vietnam government. How devastating. He was about sixty years old. Now, the reality was that he had no income, no hope, no way to get out. What would we do if we were in the same situation? Social Security, Medicare and Medicaid were absolutely fairy tales in Vietnam.

Mother passed away around April 1975 after years of illness.

The North Vietnamese captured Brother Tan and brother-in-law Lang. They became POWs.

My brothers and sisters who lived in Vietnam at that time tell incomprehensible stories of that time.

Here in the US, it was just like sitting on hot irons, every day I was at a loss. I did not know what to do.

But I had to move on. I had to find a job.

Then hope arrived. Big news. A few months after the April tragedy I received a letter from Hiep. Hiep wrote to me from a refugee camp in Asia. I remember it was Pulau Bidong camp. Hiep and Lan remember the name better than I.

There were many camps in Asia at that time. In 1975 several million people got out of Vietnam by sea or by land.

Here again, you want to watch Ken Burn's '*The War In Vietnam*' for the big picture.

Ron and I welcomed Hiep and Lan to our twelve by forty-four-foot trailer which was located in the middle of the abandoned orange grove in Thonotosassa Florida. Our trailer was just six miles from USF.

The day Hiep Lan arrived in Florida was also the day I had to be in Jacksonville Florida for my new job training and orientation as new auditor for Blue Cross of Florida.

My first job after college. My pay was ten thousand dollars a year or one hundred ninety-two dollars a week. Wow, that was good money for us. Compared to the minimum wages $2.75 an hour I earned working for the school.

Ron was still working on his master's degree at USF at that time. Now he did not to have to co-op and could concentrate on completing his degree.

1975 and the Following Years to 1982

That was a happier time for me. I saw hope that my family in Vietnam was still ok. At least for some.

Subsequently I learned that Mother passed away. How sad. How would the rest of my younger brothers and sisters and Thu live? Thu, Hai, and Luan were only about nine or ten years old.

Truong would have been eight or nine years old. Anh Thu, Thai were only two to four years older.

Hang was around seventeen and Nga around nineteen. Wow. They were all so young to navigate the grueling time in the tragedy of South Vietnam history. Sister Khanh was only around 40 years old. With several of her own children to care for. Her husband Anh Lang and our big brother Tan were Prisoners of war.

A few months later, I received a letter from France. It was a letter Nga had written. Someone in France forwarded it to me. This was what I had been looking for. In the letter Nga wrote briefly about our family situation in Vietnam. No one ever wanted to talk about the Viet Cong regime because of the potential dire consequences for the writer and family.

Nga gave me the name and address of a person in France where I could send money, and this person would forward it to Nga in Saigon.

Since that person could only accept French Franc, I went down to the bank in downtown Tampa and asked to convert some US dollars into French Francs. Every month, I sent half of my earnings to Vietnam to Nga and the other half I used for our living expenses.

I saw a lot of hope in this arrangement. At least Thu and my brothers and sisters had some resources.

At first, I did not think much about our father's situation. I thought he was always a breadwinner and could always take care of himself. How wrong I was. Halfway around the world, in 1971 when I left Vietnam I brought with me the image of our father, a strong, self-confident, and capable man. Then while mother was alive, she did not say much about him. Sometimes she would write that Father wanted to sell our house in Ngo Tung Chau Street. She asked me if she should sell it. I wrote back and advised her to sell it if that was what was needed.

1975 and the Following Years to 1982

She later on wrote that she sold the house and divided it into 50/50 for her and Father. She further said that she used the money to pay off her debts.

All the years from around 1960 to around 1975 our father lived alone and worked in Khanh Binh to earn enough money to pay for our living expenses. Mother had to be in 128/15 to take care of many of us. We, not knowing any better, took him for granted. I never thought of what he must have gone through to provide us with a comfortable life in Saigon. But the local women saw him as a golden opportunity. They, too, wanted to have a good economic life. They sought to capture this man who was alone and away from his family. After all, he had a good position. He worked for the Vietnamese government and had much authority. The South Vietnamese Government had empowered him.

That is the reality of life. This is happening right now and will continue to happen in the future. In the world of people, all living things including plants and animals strive for survival.

You see the vine climbing on a branch of the tree trying to catch sunlight to survive, to produce and to spread their own genes. No matter what the shape of the tree or the branch.

I remember once I went down to Khanh Binh for Uncle Be's little girl Xuan's funeral. I saw a woman in father's bed. Father told me not to say anything to Mother because he worried about Mother's health at that time. If she learned about this, it would only make her health worse. He also said that he was alone in Khanh Binh and many times he felt lonely and sometimes sick and there was no one around to help him. Of course, I said nothing to Mother.

I left Vietnam soon after that so the year must have been 1970.

I continued sending the help to Nga through a person in France. Each month half of my salary went to VN and half I kept for our living expenses.

Our trailer at Thonotosassa was too small for four people. Soon Hiep and Lan found a rental place nearby.

1975 and the Following Years to 1982

As refugees, new immigrants in this country, we all had to struggle when we first got here but we inherited good genes from our parents, had a good mind and the desire to be better. We all had a way to get to where we wanted.

America is still a land of opportunity for all of us. We all are very fortunate. Our parents passed on their perfect genes to each and every one of us. We are lucky compared to millions and millions of people. Who are not so lucky to be so blessed.

In 1977 Ron was hired by P&G around a year before he earned his master's degree. We moved to Cincinnati in 1978.

When we were ready for the move P&G sent a Mayflower Van to our trailer to pick up our belongings. This truck was bigger than our trailer. We had very few things for them to move. Remember, in Tampa, we were poor students. For a while Ron and I operated a garbage and trash service thanks to the step van Ron had. But then they told us we could not operate that business without a license which was very difficult to get.

Ron moved to Cincinnati first, I stayed behind to handle a few miscellaneous items. So, I moved in for a few days with Hiep and Lan at their apartment. I remember there were so many cockroaches in that apartment. The roaches crawled out a lot more at night. I told Hiep about the roaches.

In good spirit Hiep replied "Oh, not to worry, they do not eat much."

Ron's first job out of college was with P&G. We did not know much about the company but in Cincinnati, everyone we talked to often asked "who do you work for?" We would reply, Procter and Gamble and their reaction was always "that is a great company to work for."

I quit my job as an auditor for Blue Cross of Florida and moved to Cincinnati.

We stayed in our rental house at Springbrook Avenue in College Hill for 3 months. I then found a house on Archland Drive, College Hill Ohio.

1975 and the Following Years to 1982

The house was still there in 2022. It is a nice little home in a nice neighborhood. We paid $47,000 for it. We had no money, but Ron was able to get a VA home loan with just a $1000.00 down payment.

13

1978 Escaping Vietnam

One day. A day with the Lord's blessing, a short time after Thai, Hai and Luan arrived at our Archland Drive home, I received a letter that Nga sent from one of the refugee camps in Asia. Wow. Nga informed us that she was out of Vietnam. Nhuan and Nga were able to buy some 'seats' on one of those unseaworthy refugee boats to escape the Communist regime. After a long and dangerous journey, Nhuan and Nga have arrived at the camp with Thu, Lac, and Le Quyen.

What a miracle.

I heard from Nga that her escape from Vietnam was very difficult and full of challenges. Nga, Nhuan, Thu, Lac and Le Quyen had to disguise their identities and hide underneath a lower deck of a chicken carry truck. The truck transported chickens on the upper deck. The escapee was in the lower deck and at times, the chicken had poop fell on top of their heads.

I believed in miracles, somehow our family was blessed by divine power. After all of those perilous journeys. The way we went through life was full of treacherous challenges, full of life-threatening periods and many times with very grave conditions and yet we are still here.

At that time, I immediately wrote a letter to the US Embassy at Malaysia, Indonesia. In the letter, just like the previous one I wrote for Thai, Hai, and Luan, I informed the Embassy that I a US citizen was willing to sponsor my family and that I was employed by P&G and had a steady income. Now I have come to realize that my decision of accepting a lower position with P&G was a very good decision because I was employed and had a steady income.

1978 Escaping Vietnam

Parallel to my job at P&G, I also worked with Mr. Phan Vu at the Catholic social services to complete the US Immigration Services paperwork requirements. The requirements were and still are very demanding.

In the winter of 1978-79 Nga, Nhuan, Thu, Le Quyen and Lac arrived at our home at Archland Drive.

During the time I was working to get our family members out of Vietnam, I received a letter from Mrs. Tan, Nhuan's sister. She said that she too, was picked up by some organization at the fall of Vietnam. She had settled in Orlando, Florida. She asked me about Nhuan and Nga's situation in Vietnam. We exchanged a few casual conversations over the phone.

After Nhuan and Nga arrived in Cincinnati, Mrs. Tan asked me if I would let Nhuan and Nga move to Florida where she and her family now lived. I replied to her that the decision was between Nhuan, Nga and her. The decision was not mine to make. Soon after arriving in Cincinnati, Nhuan, Nga and Le Quyen moved to Florida.

Years of My Life

I remember once Nhuan said he wished he could take Truong with him to Florida but understood he couldn't at that time. Perhaps in a few years he could. I understood Nhuan's feelings. After all, if you raise a child for a while separation is not easy.

One day, around 1978-79, yes, that one fateful day again. I received a letter from Uncle Be from Vietnam. In that letter, he informed me that Father had passed away. I remember that very moment. I was stepping down to my basement garage to get into the car to go somewhere. I stopped and stood numbed.

I did not know what to think or do. I had left Vietnam in 1971 and had often wanted to go back to see our parents and perhaps bring them to the US. I left Vietnam with the emotion of a runaway person. Runaway to freedom, to escape. Runaway from the old narrow-minded customs, cultures, and society. I ran far to find a better future where I could spread my wings and fly high. I wanted to forget all the troubles, the sorrows, the unfounded idea of 'guilt' which I thought were unfairly imposed on me.

1978 Escaping Vietnam

Ron and I now had four teenagers, Hai, Luan, Thu and Truong to raise. This was a brand-new learning for us, and I am sure it was brand new to the four kids too. We enrolled the kids first to College Hill elementary school for a short while. In Cincinnati, children go to school according to the area where they live. That is

unless parents can send the kids to private school. It is still that way in 2022.

Hiep and Lan came to visit us after Hai, Luan, Truong, and Thu arrived in the US and provided extra help for them.

A short time after that I realized College Hill Elementary school was not the place I wanted for the four to go to school. I enrolled them in the St. Vivian, which is a Catholic school near our house. St. Vivian school was where most of the neighborhood kids were attending. Our Mother was heavily influenced by the Catholic doctrine, and we all went to Catholic school in Vietnam. St. Vivian was the right choice.

At their enrollment, the school administration priest reminded me that St. Vivian was a 'private' school and tuition was very high for non-parish members. Parish members received a lower tuition rate because the children's parents made donation.

Of course, Ron and I quickly registered at St. Vivian's as parish members. We wanted to do that anyway. Thu has always been a good Catholic and often took us to Church on Sunday. Thu wanted to be baptized as an 'official' Catholic. To be a sponsor for someone to be baptized, that person must be a practicing, Christian.

We did not know anyone but only the volunteer teacher, Mrs. Peterson, who often came to our house teaching the kids English. I asked her to be Thu's sponsor, and she politely told me that the duties were immense, and she did not think she could accept that role.

We turned to Joy Miller, Gordon's wife. Gordon has been Ron's friend since the USF time. Joy said she would be honored to be Thu's Sponsor to the Catholic Church.

At St. Vivian school, the kids were placed in class according to their ages no matter what their academic background was. Hai and Luan were placed in the eighth grade. Thu was placed in the seventh grade and Truong was placed in sixth grade.

Later, Thu told us that when she was in Vietnam, she was only in second or third grade. This meant she skipped several grades to go to into the seventh grade.

Every Sunday, we all dressed up and went to St. Vivian Church. I donated, but it was not anywhere near the tuition I would have to pay if we were not parish member. One day, yes, that one day again, a St. Vivian Priest called me in for a meeting. When I came, I saw two or three priests in the meeting. One priest, probably the head of the church reminded me of my sacrament to God.

I did not know what he was talking about but later on, I figured that out. On the parish membership application there was a question about who had performed our marriage. We had answered that a 'Chaplain' had performed the marriage. Little did we know that a 'Chaplain performing the wedding ceremony' was not acceptable to the Catholic Church. So, I did not fulfill my 'sacrament to God." Another guilt imposed on me but this time, I brushed that away.

Thu, Hai, Luan, and Truong received extra English lessons at St. Vivian school. They also had speech therapy classes.

I met with several of their teachers and educational therapists, and I still have their school reports.

1978 Escaping Vietnam

Eighth grade is the highest-grade St. Vivian offers. After that, Hai and Luan went to Roger Bacon Catholic high school. After Thu completed seventh grade, she moved to eighth grade, and Truong, seventh grades.

Raising the four teenagers without any prior experience was a learning experience for both Ron and me. I am sure, it was also a challenging experience for the kids to learn to live with us.

Ron and I made sure the kids were enrolled in all the neighborhood ball teams and attended the games they played. We donated soft drinks and treats to their teammates. The kids helped with chores around the house.

Kurt was born on November 25, 1981, while we were living at 1068 Archland. Ron had to travel very often for his job with P&G. I was home with all the kids most of the time. Soon, the house was too small for all of us, so we needed a bigger place. Additionally, we needed a better school district than Cincinnati.

We moved to Rexford Drive, Evendale Ohio in 1982. Hai, Luan, and Thu all graduated from Princeton High School while we lived at Rexford Drive. Truong was in eleventh grade.

1978 Escaping Vietnam

Years of My Life

14

1982-1986 Evandale – Indian Hill

We lived in our house on Rexford Drive, Evendale Ohio. This is a nice neighborhood just outside Cincinnati. Children in this neighborhood attend the Princeton school district. Before moving there, I checked with parents whose children were attending Princeton high school. These parents expressed their satisfaction with the academic learning their children received at this school.

Surrounding our home was still a lot of farmlands. Murphy Builder built our Archland home. Murphy has a good reputation of building a good solid home within a reasonable price. Our house was a typical home with four bedrooms and two and a half baths.

The mortgage interest rate was very high at 14.5%. Nobody was buying houses at that time. We bought our house at a very good price and without a real-estate broker involved.

I continued to work with Mr. Phan Vu and the Catholic Social Services supplying him with paperwork the US Immigration required for Anh Tan, Chi Khanh, Hang, Thuy, Anh Thu, and their family members. Everyone was still stuck in Vietnam. The country was poor and in very harsh economic condition as a result of many years at war and a trade embargo by the US.

The Vietnamese Refugees without US family sponsors were being spread out to any country that would take them. Those without a sponsor or not accepted by any non-communist countries would be sent back to Vietnam.

Mr. Vu recognized the size of our family and occasionally said that I was bringing out the whole Vietnam country.

Ron and I definitely wanted all of our family here in the US.

1982-1986 Evandale – Indian Hill

At P&G, I got promoted to the management rank. I was assigned to the Chemicals Division and worked in downtown Cincinnati in twin tower north (TN-12.) This location was great because I could walk to the Catholic Social Services and work with Mr. Vu.

Around 1985-86 Hai, Luan, and Thu graduated from Princeton High. They were busy with graduation and High school dance night. I bought suites for Hai and Luan to wear to their graduation. Thu had a beautiful dress to wear for the dance night. I knew graduation was a celebration event but that was still a new idea to me.

You see. We all are creatures familiar with our background and how we grew up. We all have our past as our reference. At times we do not recognize that some of our past ideas are obsolete and need to be changed. I was a child growing up in the poor country of Vietnam. I had had numerous academic achievements even when I was a small child. Our parents were very busy with making a living. They overlooked their children's achievements and celebration events.

I remember while I was in third grade and our family was living in Rach Gia, when my third-grade academic year end and at the graduation celebration event, I walked up to the podium at the town hall which was filled with other kids parents and town dignitaries to receive my academic excellence award with none of my parents in the audience. Father was busy earning a living in Khanh Binh and Mother had many, many, kids to care for. I was seven or eight years old. I think I understood the reality and accepted it without thinking and with no reservations.

The Vietnamese have an old saying "Children of the King will be Kings; Children of the Monks will stay in the pagoda to sweep the leaves of the banyan trees." I think this saying influenced our mother more than our father. Because whenever I wished for something that maybe was out of our reach, she would say that quote or something similar.

But for me I could not accept this. I always wanted to reach for the blue sky and often said to myself, "When I grow up, I will follow my dreams."

1982-1986 Evandale – Indian Hill

Soon we realized that we needed to move on to a bigger and better place than the current home at 9666 Rexford Drive.

The neighborhood next to our Rexford house was still farmland. One of the Murphy children, Bob Murphy, was living in that farmhouse. Hai worked there sometimes as a helper. That is how we get to know Bob.

Then I read in the local paper about a five-acre lot in Indian Hill for sale. I recognized that if we sold our Rexford house, we could buy this Indian Hill lot. I advertised the sale of our home. I sold the house by myself quickly because it was a well-built home, and it was only 4 years old. We made a nice profit from the sale.

Since we already had a five-acre lot, I contacted Bob Murphy and had him build our current home on Hopewell Road. With the accounting head in me, and with the spreadsheet in front of me, I did several what-if scenarios and calculated that with both Ron's and my income we could barely afford this Indian Hill home. But if we had to sell it, we would make a nice profit.

I worked with Bob Murphy to build our current home. It took Bob ten months to complete.

Ron was very handy. He fixed up the cottage so we could live in it while the main house was being built. The previous owner wanted to destroy this cottage but now look at it. It has been home for many brothers and sisters and their families. Now Ron uses it as his writing castle.

We moved in and settled in our current home in the Village of Indian Hill, Ohio in October 1986. This is a very beautiful neighborhood with a lot of green trees and open space.

Thu, Hai, and Luan graduated from Princeton High school and got accepted to The Ohio State University, Columbus, Ohio.

Truong at first moved with us but he was not happy with Indian Hill high school and decided to move back to the Princeton High area by himself.

1982-1986 Evandale – Indian Hill

Ron and I were still working for P&G. I got promoted to the management rank, but our combined income was still very low, and we continue to struggle to pay our mortgage, living expenses, childcare and other bills. I still needed to work and have a steady income. No one should ever underestimate the power of a steady income.

Derek was born on November 19, 1987. I was now a working mother of two small children holding a full-time job.

Finding childcare was a challenge. I often felt guilty about leaving my young children for someone to care of while I went to work.

Every morning, I was up at five in the morning to get ready for the day. At 6 AM, I would wake up Kurt and Derek. Then I would prepare them to go to school or day care.

1982-1986 Evandale – Indian Hill

I remember when Derek was about two years old and Kurt was eight everyday about 7:15 am, I would put them in the car seats and dropped Derek off first at Children's Corner then I would take Kurt to Indian Hill Elementary school to drop him off before going to work.

The Indian Hill elementary school did not open until after 8AM. Many days we got there early. I would drop Kurt off then sit in the parking lot watching him until the school opened.

Then I drove to downtown Cincinnati to P&G TN2.

I was often late for work. Back in those days, employers were not "friendly" to working mothers. They expected working mothers to earn "their keep" just like the men. There was no such thing as "working from home." God forbid if your child got sick and you could not find a place or a person to care for your sick child.

When I arrived at P&G downtown, I took the freight elevator that was usually empty, which started from the basement tunnel and land in the back office of TN12. I always hoped that nobody would catch me being late. I would enter like a church mouse, and carefully slide into my cubicle at TN12. Usually that was 9AM. I was always thirty minutes late.

To make up for those thirty minutes, I would leave my office at 5pm and not 4.30pm.

That of course made me hurry to the daycare to pick up Derek. The daycare had a strict pickup time requirement. The children had to be picked up by 5.30 pm. No later than that because working staff had their own lives too.

1982-1986 Evandale – Indian Hill

Most of the time, I was at the daycare right at closing time. Traffic on I-71 was as crowded then as it is now.

After I picked up Derek and Kurt, I took them home and fixed dinner for them.

Ron helped when he was not travelling.

The next day, everything started over.

Thuy, Hang, Anh Thu, and Anh Tan, sister Khanh and all members of their families were still in Vietnam. It had now been nine or ten years since the fall of South Vietnam. Our family history, Vietnam history and the world history has been, will be intertwined for many decades from now. In my recollections I am trying to talk about the events that affected our family.

Of course, I can only talk from my perspective and experience. I am sure all the sisters and brothers have their own circumstances, knowledge, and feelings to express.

During those intervening decades millions and millions of people tried to escape Vietnam to avoid the North Vietnam regime's punishments.

Many still poured out to the ocean in the unseaworthy boats and under horrific conditions. They tried to escape Vietnam with a slim hope to find freedom, opportunities and to avoid the slow death. The world news showed many tragedies. Many people lost their lives due to the ocean violent storms or the pirates seized the opportunity to attack the refugees, rob them, kill them, and rape the women, taking advantage of the defenseless.

In our family, Anh Tan and Anh Lang were captured by the communist and sent to their re-education camps.

They were POWs for eight to ten years. I remember some fragmented stories Anh Tan and Anh Lang told me about the time they were in prison. Sister Khanh also told me some of her difficult stories. She is the wife of a POW that has relatives in the US. Recently I visited my sister Khanh in Florida and talked to her about her experience. I recorded her story.

1982-1986 Evandale – Indian Hill

How I wish I had talked more to Anh Tan about his POW experience. Anh Lang talked about one day in the camp, he was so hungry he stole a potato and hit it under his shirt in front of his stomach until now he still has that scar.

During this time the US Politicians, being the sore losers imposed economic sanction on Vietnam. You can imagine the situation of most poor Vietnamese when the almighty Washington politicians heartlessly determined their economic life. Their blood life.

The United Nation High Commissioner for Refugees intervened in the situation in Vietnam because they realized that the innocent cannot keep on pouring out to the ocean or the neighboring countries. Poor Asian countries cried for help, they could not accept millions and millions of refugees. The refugee's lives were also in danger. The UNHCR worked with the US, the Vietnamese government, and the neighboring countries on the Orderly Departure Program (ODP).

Looking at the world geography map one will see that the countries surrounding Vietnam are not the rich or powerful countries. It was natural that they could not handle the hundred thousand or million refugees pouring into their countries. The Asian Countries simply do not have the resources, the desires to handle this ocean of refugees.

Few of those refugees had relatives in the US or in Europe to sponsor them.

A million people went to Hong Kong, Malaysia, Indonesia and stayed in limbo for years at the refugee camps and many were sent back to Vietnam.

I had completed the immigration paperwork for all of my brothers and sisters and their families which were still in Vietnam at that time. I submitted the applications to the Immigration office in downtown Cincinnati. I had come to that office so often with paperwork upon paperwork requirements that the Immigration employees recognized me.

1982-1986 Evandale – Indian Hill

I put down the names of all my brothers, sisters, nieces, and nephews. I gave a stack of file copies to Mr. Phan Vu at the Catholic Social Services for him to work on the refugee settlements requirements. Mr. Vu was astonished with the amount of paperwork I gave him and the number of relatives I sponsored. As I mentioned previously, in good spirit, Vu often said 'Hien, you are bringing the whole country out of Vietnam.'

I understood according to the Orderly Departure Program the Vietnamese refugees would be allowed to leave Vietnam according to their priority. They would fly out of Vietnam legally and not have to risk their lives at the sea. Those with the highest priority were the ones with US sponsors and the POW's they had the H-O status issued by the US State Department. All of these procedures needed a few years to complete because of the many requirements.

I also made sure that all my brothers, sisters and their children had a US citizen sponsor, so their priority was higher than those without relatives. Immigration laws allowed this priority.

Nhuan recalled the story of he, Nga, LeQuyen, Thu and Lac escaping Vietnam and the time he was in the refugee camp. Nhuan said that he did not know why he Nga and the kids were called very early out to enter the US. He had thought that the high-ranking Vietnamese officers such as the military Generals or full Colonels would have that priority but Nhuan, Nga and the kids had even higher priority than the ones that once were placed in the 'privileged' class.

Years later I learned the reason for this priority from an Immigration officer. Because Thu was included in the Nhuan and Nga family group. Thu was classified as an American citizen. She was underage and automatically became a US Citizen when I was naturalized. The US was taking care of and protecting their citizens first.

Sister Khanh and Anh Lang family was the first family to get out of Vietnam around the late 1988-89. I do not remember the exact year. They temporarily stayed with Ron and I at our house on Hopewell Road.

1982-1986 Evandale – Indian Hill

Around the early 1990's Hang and Dung, Anh Thu, Vi and Trang arrived. I remember one summer evening I received a phone call from someone at Cincinnati Airport. That person told me that there was a group of people waiting for me to pick them up. I wondered who those people could be.

I remember a few weeks earlier I had information about the departure date of Hang, Dung, Anh Thu, Trang and Vi. That was much later in the month. Anxiously, I did not know who was at the airport, but I drove to CVG anyway.

When I arrived at the airport, I saw my two sisters and their children sitting on the high rising stone platform. They were small, frail, their clothing was worn. Everyone looked so small and frail. Life in Vietnam was not easy. Dung was small, Vi was also small but Trang was very tiny, so tiny-tiny.

It was a very emotional moment. They were here at last. After years of hard work getting through all the channels, I had learned my way through.

They were now finally in the land of opportunities. In the land where they could achieve their dreams of going to college, to fly high in a much and much easier country than if they were still in Vietnam.

Here, they have the support and encouragement of family, the US government, the ease of abundant opportunities, and resources.

I could not imagine the life of single mothers with small children in Vietnam. It is almost impossible to have a decent life in Vietnam, a country which is not only very poor but also with double standards.

1982-1986 Evandale – Indian Hill

It was very harsh on women in all aspects of the society. Almost all the doors from economic condition, education, thinking, and many other opportunities would be shut to women with young children and no husbands.

Drawing from my own life experience while I was in Vietnam, at the time when the old Vietnam regime was in power. Our family worked and supported that regime. Life of a single mothers was extremely difficult. Now the political situation has changed completely. We are on the 'other side' where normal life is possible.

I am sure, in the other world, our parents are happier now. They see that their children, grandchildren have a great start. Our parents are still with all of us and watch over us all the time. Even to this day. Miracles are many times disguised as troubles at first. But miracles will be here at last.

Both Ron and I anxiously awaited the arrival of the rest of our family. Anh Tan and his family, Chi Tan My Co and Trinh, Thuy and his family, Hue, Khoa, Quang and Kim Ngan.

I also sponsored Anh Tan's first group of children Phuong, Diem and Toan but I was informed that they chose to stay in Vietnam.

Yes, even to this day, 2022, here in the US, everyone can have a chance to achieve the life they want and can fly as far as their desires take them. This is the reason why people still risk their lives coming to the US.

Nhuan and Nga drove up from Orlando to join us welcoming the arrival of Hang, Anh Thu, and the kids.

Later, Nga and Nhuan took Hang and Dung with them for Hang anh Dung to be settled in Florida.

For a long time, Thuy and I exchanged ideas about Thuy and his family whether to live in Vietnam or to leave for the US. I read one of Thuy's letters to Ron in which Thuy said something like this "I wish I had an ax that would allow me to can feed my family." That statement touched Ron, and he still remembers it to this day.

Thuy, at times, expressed his philosophical ideas about life in general. I think he was probably wondering just like the character Hamlet who famously said, "To be or not to be, that is the question."

1982-1986 Evandale – Indian Hill

I advised Thuy, "In the US, our children will have a better life. Think of the kids and come here." I am so happy that a short while later, Thuy and Hue arrived in the US with Khoa, Quang and Kim Ngan.

A few years later, Anh Tan, Chi Tan and their children Trinh and My Co also arrived at Cincinnati.

In October 1986 we moved to our current Hopewell Road home where we still live. We are retired here. I love living here. It is the most beautiful area of all the places I lived and visited.

Years of My Life

About Myself

I am a time traveler. I have experienced the life, the culture, the technological and geographical changes that any time traveler would experience. I began my journey on a Christmas day at a birthing midwife's thatched hut. As a young child I experienced living under a thatched roof and sleeping on a blanket on a dirt floor.

As I grew, I experienced the impact of the French domination of the Vietnamese. The patriotic Vietnamese fighters defeated the French. However, events for the Vietnamese ended up with the US getting involved after Vietnam was split in two at the 17th parallel. The North Vietnamese ended up fighting the Americans and it became the American war in Vietnam.

As a young girl I and my family moved as refugees from the North to the South of Vietnam. I then began my journey in a new culture. My mother and father supported their children and encouraged education. Khanh and I split our time between going to school and babysitting some of our siblings. We got the privilege of going to school but missed most of our childhood play years.

I excelled in school and repeatedly moved up the educational ladder. I was the first girl in my family to pass the Baccalaureate Diploma. If I had been a boy, I would have qualified to enter a military academy similar to West Point.

Years of My Life

My independent nature drove me to get a job so that I could take care of myself and help my family.

The desire for a better life for myself, my child and the rest of my family drove me to seek a way out of Vietnam. I managed to get a visa to go to school in the US.

The journey in the US at times did not go exactly as planned but I continued to strive to get my education and a job that would allow me to help my family financially and perhaps provide a way to get them out of Vietnam. Several events happened that put me in an upward but hidden path.

I met Ron Mueller and married him while in college.

I graduated and got a very good job as a Medicare Hospital examiner.

Then South Vietnam fell to the North Vietnamese.

My family went from living a normal life to being outcasts with no jobs and no income.

Two military officer brothers were imprisoned by the North Vietnamese.

I was devastated because I had been on a journey expecting to be able to get my family out. This journey took on a very different path.

I sent love, encouragement, and financial resources to support my family. I put in all the legal paperwork for all family members to help get them out.

The initial exit for many of the family was to escape by boat.

About Myself

Years later that paperwork for legal exit provided a way for the rest of the family to make their journey to the US.

So, my journey to date took me from a dirt floor, to having electricity in my home. From being a single teen mother, to earning a college education in the US, becoming a US citizen, and experiencing all the technologies of the twentieth and twenty first century.

I am a dreamer and a time traveler.

"The future belongs to those who have a dream"

Years of My Life

Published by: Around the World Publishing LLC.

QR Links to
ATWP.US web site

www.ingramcontent.com/pod-product-compliance
Lightning Source LLC
Chambersburg PA
CBHW040720170426
43209CB00046B/1722